Wellington and the Invasion of France

Volume II

Wellington and the Invasion of France

VOLUME II
The Crossing of the Bidassoa and
the Battle of the Nivelle, 1813

F. C. Beatson

LEONAUR

Wellington and the Invasion of France Volume II:
The Crossing of the Bidassoa and the Battle of the Nivelle, 1813
by F. C. Beatson

Published by Leonaur Ltd

First published 1931

ISBN: 978-1-84677-293-1 (hardcover)
ISBN: 978-1-84677-294-8 (softcover)

http://www.leonaur.com

Contents

Preface to the 1931 Edition

In September, 1813, the Allied Army, commanded by Wellington, stood on the frontier of France within the area covered by the river and estuary of the Bidassoa and the heights on its right bank.

At this period it was the desire of the British Government that Wellington should advance into France. It was hoped that such a move would spur the Allied Powers in northern Europe to closer combination and greater activity, prevent Napoleon from calling reinforcements from the large force of veteran soldiers he still had in southern France, and would also bring a large and wealthy area under Wellington's control.

In this book an attempt is made to show how a great British soldier carried out the wishes of his government and, dealing with two operations, one a brilliant success, the other only a partial one, to give, as far as can now be traced from his correspondence and other sources, the facts and reasons on which the Commander's plans were formed and executed.

It will doubtless be said: "What is the interest or use of reading or studying events which took place more than a century ago? Science and Invention have changed the world since then." But is this quite true? Let us see what great Masters say. Napoleon's opinion was thus expressed: "The science of strategy is only to be acquired by experience and by studying the campaigns of all the great Captains; this is the only way of acquiring the secret of the art of war. What was the opinion of his present-day disciple, F. Foch, the great Marshal of both France and Great Britain? In his opinion, though war has now at its disposal means more powerful and more delicate, yet the same laws as of old must be obeyed: "Forms evolve; directing principles remain unaltered."

To living Authors and Publishers of works quoted I tender my grateful acknowledgments, especially to the historical section of the French War Ministry for permission to quote from the articles on the Campaign published in 1812—13 in the *Revue d'Histoire* and written by Capitaine Vidal de la Blache; also to the Committee of the *Oxfordshire and Buckinghamshire Light Infantry Chronicle* for permission to quote from the *Chronicle* and *Moorsom's Historical Record of the 52nd Regiment.*

F. C. Beatson

CHAPTER 1

On the Border of France

It has been said very truly that the record of any historical period should bring the reader back into the atmosphere and positions of those whose actions are described. To do so he must know the circumstances in which they acted, and, so far as can be ascertained, the reasons which led them to the decisions on which their actions were based.

When dealing, as in this case, with the episodes of a campaign the reader must be given such information as will enable him to visualize the existing situation and the events which led up to it. Moreover, as war in 1813 was an act of policy he must also be acquainted with the political situation so far as it bears on the actions of the opposing commanders. The necessary information therefore may be given under two heads, the military and the political.

To take the military situation first. On Sunday, 21st June, 1813, the French army under Joseph Bonaparte, the "intrusive" King of Spain, was decisively defeated at Vitoria by the allied army under Wellington, and was driven with the loss of most of its war material and transport into France, where it arrived by various routes in a state of disorganization and confusion, and also, mainly owing to its lack of transport, in a state of almost starvation.

The news of the victory at Vitoria reached London on the 3rd July, and was received with delight and enthusiasm. In this excited state of public opinion it is not surprising that extravagant expectations arose regarding the operations of Wellington's army.[1] They (the newspaper editors), he said, "have long expected me in Bordeaux... but you may depend on this that I shall never myself form, nor encourage in others, extravagant expectations."[2]

On receipt of the news of the victory, the British Government was called on to decide on what general military policy their army in the Peninsula was to continue to operate. The decision was expressed in the following instructions sent on the 5th July by the Foreign Secretary to Lord Cathcart, Ambassador to Russia, then at the headquarters of the allied Russian and Prussian armies.

"You will inform the Emperor (Alexander) that it is the intention of His Majesty's Government, in the event of the enemy being expelled from Spain, actively to employ the allied armies on that side of" France in such a manner as will best serve to occupy the attention and military resources of the enemy, and thereby to favour the exertions of the allies in other parts of Europe."

Having thus decided, the Government informed Wellington, gave him formal authority to enter France and make such requisitions as he considered necessary for the service of the allied army under his command: and wisely left their trusted commander in the field to plan and carry out the military operations necessary to give effect to the policy.

By the end of the first week in July not a French soldier remained in north-western Spain, with the exception of the beleaguered garrisons of San Sebastian, Pamplona and Santona. Wellington had now to decide whether or not he would follow the French army into France. He decided not to do so for the present. His reasons were twofold, military and political, and it seems best that they should be discussed separately.

---

1. *Larpent's Journal,* 21st August, 1813. "Major Fremantle came back j just in time for dinner yesterday (at Lord Wellington's table) and amused us all with your madness in England about the Battle of Vitoria."
2. Wellington to Lord Bathurst, Secretary of State for War.

The first was the danger to the right flank, the rear, and the communications with the coast depots of a force composed of four divisions and a cavalry division of the army of the north under General Clausel, behind whom were the armies of Aragon and Catalonia under Marshal Suchet. Napoleon in the instructions and remonstrances he addressed to his brother during the early months of 1813 concerning his conduct of military affairs warned him of the danger of leaving Suchet's forces outside the scope of his own operations, and ordered him to maintain a short and secure line of communication with the Marshal. King Joseph did neither.

On the other hand Wellington, with as clear an insight into the general situation as the Emperor, saw that for the success of his own operations Suchet must by all possible means be prevented from combining with Joseph. As Napier says, "his (Wellington's) wings were Spread for a long flight," and he had no wish to find the King's armies reinforced by Suchet's troops, or these latter threatening his right flank from the Ebro valley. Therefore Suchet must be kept fully occupied in his own area and tied if possible to the eastern coast.

To effect this the means at Wellington's disposal were an Anglo-Sicilian force of about 11,000 men, 9,000 of whom were British and two bodies of Spanish troops paid and equipped by Britain, and commanded by British officers. The whole, numbering about 17,000 men, were under the command of Lieutenant-General Sir John Murray. Wellington's general plan was that the French should be gradually drawn northwards by operations against their communications, power to do so being with the allies as they had command of the sea, Murray having a flotilla of transports and the full support of the British Mediterranean fleet.

To draw Suchet from Valencia Murray was ordered to embark at least 10,000 men and lay siege to Tarragona, a fortress on the east coast between the mouth of the Ebro and Barcelona. On 2nd June Murray landed about 14,000 men and invested the place. Suchet, rightly judging that the aim of the expedition was a landing on the Catalonian Coast, marched north. Hearing of Suchet's move, Murray, who would give his confidence to no one, even his second-in-command, or the admiral, lost all confidence in himself. After changing his plans and orders several times, he determined to raise the siege and re-embark his force, which he did on the night of 12/13th June, when the French columns, which had not yet joined hands, were over 30 miles distant. The siege train—"the guns that shook the bloody ramparts of Badajoz"—was left behind, and the army to its mortification and disgust saw them carried unto the fortress by the garrison. A few days later it was decided to re-embark the troops. Hardly however had the decision been come to than the main division of the fleet arrived, and with it, to the delight of the troops, came Lord William Bentinck to resume command of the troops.

Wellington received the news of Murray's failure about the 1st July. Meanwhile Clausel, who was under orders to rejoin the main army at Vitoria, had reached Tevino, about 8 miles south of Vitoria, on the 22nd June. Here he learnt of the battle from the country people and halting sent a strong cavalry patrol to verify the information. On the return of the cavalry he immediately retreated southwards, intending to cross the mountains and join the King, to whom he dispatched a letter in cipher,[1] and reached Logrono where he remained until the 25th. Having received confused information of the allied movements, Clausel marched from Logrono on the evening of the 25th, and by a wonderful march of 60 miles in 40 hours arrived at Tudela on the 27th.

1. Clausel to King Joseph, 23rd June. "Sire, I moved yesterday to within half a league of Vitoria by the road from Guardia. If I learn that your Majesty is at Salvatierra or in the Araquil valley I will move there. If not I will march towards Pamplona."

Clausel's letter to King Joseph fell into Wellington's hands, who was now with the greater part of his army about Pamplona. On the information it contained he hoped by a move southwards to cut off Clausel before he could reach Tudela. Leaving Hill with the 2nd, the Portuguese Division and Morillo's Spaniards to invest Pamplona, Wellington with the 3rd, 4th, 7th and light divisions moved towards Tafalla, whilst the 5th and 6th Divisions marched from Salvatierra and Vitoria towards Logrono, and Mina, who had concentrated at Estella with about 10,000 infantry and 1,000 of Julian Sauchez's cavalry, was also ordered to make for Tudela.

But, as we have seen, Clausel had reached Tudela on the 27th; leaving there on the 28th and taking its garrison with him he moved towards Zaragoza where he arrived on the 30th June. Wellington, whose movements were retarded by the badness of the roads and heavy rain, made a corresponding march to Caseda, aiming to cut off Clausel from the road into France by Jaca and the Somport Pass, but here he gave up the pursuit and returned to Pamplona.

Clausel remained at Zaragoza until the 3rd July, when, having no news of Joseph's army, he decided to move northwards to Jaca, where he would be able, either to join the main army, or Suchet, if the latter moved up the Ebro valley. Leaving his artillery and Paris's brigade of the army of Aragon in Zaragoza he reached Jaca on the 6th July.

Meanwhile Mina continued his pursuit, and on the 9th approached Zaragoza. Paris, who had been ordered by Suchet to retire to Caspe[1]—an order given by Suchet on the assumption that Clausel would remain at Zaragoza— also decided to move to Jaca. Leaving a garrison of 500 men in the citadel, he left Zaragoza on the evening of the 10th, and reached Jaca on the 13th July, being followed all the way by a column of Mina's force, which hung closely on his rear, and caused him considerable losses.

---

1. In the Ebro valley about 80 miles south of Zaragoza.

Clausel heard on the 11th July that Paris had left Zaragoza, which signified that he was now cut off from Suchet's armies; he moved from Jaca into France by the Somport Pass and reached St. Jean Pied-de-Port on the 16th July. On the 30th July the citadel of Zaragoza surrendered to Mina. When news of this reached Paris, he also retreated into France, leaving a garrison of 750 men in the fort of Jaca, and arrived at Urdos in the Valley D'aspe with about 2,500 men on the 12th August. On Paris's departure Jaca was invested by the Spaniards. Thus was abandoned the only remaining tract of country which, if held, offered facilities for the junction of Soult's and Suchet's armies.

When the news of the allied victory at Vitoria reached Marshal Suchet, who knew that Clausel was at Zaragoza, he determined to move there in order to secure a point where the army of Aragon could join that of King Joseph, if the latter could re-enter Spain, and fixed Caspe as the concentration point of his army. By the 12th Suchet's force was distributed along the Ebro from Caspe to Tortosa. Now, however, came the news that Clausel had abandoned Zaragoza and that Mina and all his partisan bands were closing on the City. Suchet ordered Paris to retreat to Caspe, gave up his intention of moving on Zaragoza, and finding he could not feed his army about Tortosa, he crossed the Ebro on 15th July and moving by Tarragona took up a strong position at Villafranca some 15 miles to the west of Barcelona.

So, for the time being at any rate, the threat to the left flank of the allied army was removed.

Another reason for Wellington's decision was the state and the wants of his army at this time. That army "which in six weeks had marched 600 miles, passed six great rivers and gained one decisive victory"[1] and "had started in the highest order, and could not have done better than it did up to and during the battle"[2] had, owing to victory, plunder, rain and

1. Napier: *History of the Peninsular War.*
2. Wellington to Bathurst, Caseda, 29th June, 1813.

fatigue, temporarily lost itself. It required some rest and time to pull itself together again.

Moreover, its wants were many. The reserves of musket ammunition had been so depleted that the French ammunition captured at Vitoria had to be issued to the troops, notwithstanding that the calibre of the French musket was smaller than that of the British. The soldiers were badly off for shoes,[1] and there was a general want of stores and necessaries owing to the store ships, which had been loaded and ready to sail from Lisbon oh the 12th May, being still there on the 19th June, and the military stores and provisions which Wellington expected to find at Santander did not arrive there until early in July, owing to the want of, or the misuse of, the naval force to protect the convoys. The organization of the newly formed depots on the coast of Biscay needed attention and their communication required to be assured.

On military grounds Wellington decided not to advance immediately.

THE POLITICAL SITUATION AND THE DISTRIBUTION OF THE ALLIED ARMY IN GERMANY

Of that great army of over half a million men which Napoleon in June, 1812, had led across the Niemen to invade Russia there staggered across the Prussian frontier in December but a remnant of wounded, frost-bitten starving men, a mob not an army.

One result of this disastrous ending to Napoleon's venture was to crack, if not to break, the spell of his domination of Germany. At this time the only great Powers at war with France were Great Britain and Russia. Prussia and Austria were allied to France by the treaty of March, 1812, which bound each of them to furnish 30,000 men to operate un-

---

1. Wellington to Bathurst, 12th July, 1813. "If they (the enemy) take the ship with our shoes, we must halt for six weeks."

der Napoleon's orders. As soon as Yorck, who commanded the Prussian contingent then with Macdonald's corps in the Riga district, became aware of the actual state of affairs, he concluded an arrangement with the Russian Commander which neutralized his contingent for the time being. Shortly afterwards Schwartzenberg, in command of the Austrians, followed Yorck's example and withdrew his force to Cracow.

Meanwhile, as the news of the French disaster spread through Prussia, a wave of enthusiasm for the liberation of the country from the heavy yoke of French domination spread throughout Prussia. The King, having proceeded to Breslau, concluded a treaty with the Emperor Alexander, whereby both Powers were to conduct a war against France conjointly, and Russia agreed not to lay down arms until Prussia received back the provinces of which Napoleon had deprived her. On the 17th March, 1813, Prussia declared war against France. All classes rushed to join the Colours. Old men gave their money and women their jewels.

Thus in March all the great Powers except Austria were at war with France. Although Austria had withdrawn her troops from the French army, she remained an ally by virtue of the 1812 treaty. There was, however, a strong party in the country desirous of taking advantage of the state of the French army and joining the coalition. But Metternich, the Chancellor of the Empire, though he shared the views of this party, considered the time was not yet ripe for a decided break with France, and that for the present Austria's interests would be best served by maintaining as far as possible a neutral attitude and acting as a mediator between the opponents.

Austria was the Power which in reality held the balance between the fairly equal opposing forces, had her own objects to gain and had no wish to see any of the Powers gaining territory outside their natural limits. The longer she remained neutral the higher would be the price of her alliance, and Metternich was determined that this would go to that side which would give the best price.

To this end Austria began to offer her services as mediator.[1] Both Napoleon and Great Britain refused to accept them: the former because he was forming a new army and meant to use it; the latter because the British Government considered there was little likelihood of any peace being permanent until Napoleon was totally overthrown. Further offers were made but were again declined and Austria began to strengthen her army.

During this period Napoleon, who had left his army after the crossing of the Beresina, had reached Paris on the 18th December, and was putting all his energy and organizing skill into the formation of a new army. By the beginning of April its various corps were on their way from France and Italy towards the line of the River Saale, behind which was Prince Eugene Beauharnais[2] with about 70,000 men, the remnants of the *grande armee* together with reinforcements which had reached him from time to time.

But this army was not the equal of its predecessors; most of the veterans of Austerlitz, Jena and Wagram lay beneath the snow of the plains of Russia. France had been bled by the conscription, which now produced more boys than men. It was weak in cavalry as there was not time to train men and horses, but Napoleon took care to make it as strong as possible in artillery, knowing well that "the more inferior the quality of the troops the more artillery is necessary." [3] It had another weakness in that it lacked the backbone of an army, trained officers and non-commissioned officers.

---

1. *Cambridge Modern History,* Vol. IX, Napoleon. "By the middle of April Austria ceased to be an ally of France and had begun to mediate as an independent power."
2. Napoleon before leaving his army handed over the command to Murat, King of Naples, who at Posen on 16th January proposed to hand it over to Prince Eugene. The reply of the latter was: "You cannot make it over to me, only the Emperor can do that, but you can run away in the night, and the supreme command will devolve on me the next morning," and Murat departed that day for Naples.
3. Napoleon to Clarke, 18th August, 1813.

On the 25th April Napoleon joined his army at Erfurt, its strength being about 200,000 men. By this time the Russian and Prussian armies had advanced into Saxony, being about 85,000 strong. It is unnecessary here to go into any details of the campaign which followed. It will suffice to say that Napoleon issuing forth from the screen of the Saale, seized Leipzig, drove the allies eastward through Dresden, whence they retired to Bautzen on the Spree, where they made a stand; Napoleon attacked on the 2ist May and seized the river line and the town, the allies retreating to Bunzlau and Lowenberg. Having reached this line they decided not to continue their retreat any further in a direct easterly direction, but to wheel to the south and move towards Schweidnitz.

When information of this change of direction reached Napoleon at Liegnitz he decided on an operation which, if carried out, would have equalled his greatest previous victories. It was to follow the retreating allies with two of his corps only while the rest of the army moved to Breslau on the Oder, from whence it was to move by Strehlen beyond the allied left wing.

> "Thus he would again, as so often before, have turned the enemy strategically, for being in possession of the line of the Oder and attacking with his main body from Breslau the allied communications behind Schweidnitz, he could force them back against the Eulengebirge mountains and annihilate them."[1]

But now came a surprise. Notwithstanding his commanding position both as regards numbers and position, Napoleon on the 26th May sent General. Caulaincourt to the allied headquarters with proposals for an armistice. The outcome of the negotiations was that on the 1st June an armistice commencing on the 2nd June and lasting till the 20th July, with six days of grace, was concluded at Plaswitz. On 20th June, after Met-

---

1 *Napoleon as a General,* Count Yorck von Watenburg, Vol. II.

ternich had had an interview with Napoleon at Dresden, the armistice was extended to the 10th August, and a convention agreed to that a congress should assemble at Prague to settle the terms of a general peace.

Napoleon stated his reasons for desiring an armistice as follows: "I decided for it on two grounds:—first, because of my want of cavalry which prevented me from dealing great blows, and secondly because of the hostile attitude of Austria."[1] According to Jomini, it was his greatest mistake. It is probable that none of the Powers desired peace; it was time they all wanted.

On the 1st July Napoleon received the first report of the Battle of Vitoria. He did all he could to suppress the news, but effective steps had been taken in London to inform the Powers and make it generally known on the continent.[2] On 12th July it reached the allied Monarchs and its effect was immediate and powerful. "The impression of the allies," says Sir C. Stewart, the British representative at the headquarters of the Prussian army, "was strong and universal, and produced ultimately, in my opinion, the recommencement of hostilities." [3]

The news of the armistice of Plaswitz and the agreement to hold a conference was conveyed to Wellington in a letter of 23rd June from the Secretary of State, in which Lord Bathurst expressed the opinion that it was unlikely that it would enable

---

1. Napoleon to Clarke (Minister of War), Newmarket, 2nd June, 1813.
2. Liverpool to Wellington, 3rd July. Croker to Wellington: "We are dispatching your Gazette in French, Dutch and German to all corners of Europe." In the archives de Guerre in Paris is a copy, which a British cruiser obliged French fishermen off the coast of Fecamp to take on 8th July, 1813.
3. Count Nugent to Wellington. Prague, 27th July, 1813: "The action (Vitoria) is acknowledged by everyone to be the most glorious of the whole twenty years' war, and besides its importance as regards Spain, it is far more so by its influence on the state of affairs here. The account of the state of affairs in Spain and your plans, in short everything you desired me to say, has had the greatest effect and contributed to the decision of Austria, and the Battle of Vitoria, I think, settled the matter."

Napoleon to send any reinforcements intended for Germany to the French army of Spain owing to the critical situation of his own army. He states however that:

> . . . . the last accounts from the allies are not so sanguine as they have been. I saw a private letter to Munster from Vienna which impresses me with little hope of any real goodwill, and almost none of any manly decision—the worst was the jealousies amongst the generals, and the want of any person whom all would gladly obey.

Wellington naturally had to consider what the effect might be on his own position. If the result was a general peace he had nothing to be anxious about, and nothing was to be gained by an advance into France and having to retire therefrom when peace was proclaimed. If, however, the peace was confined to France, Prussia and Russia, the Powers then actually at war in northern Europe, Great Britain and Spain would be exposed to the full military power of France. This result was perhaps unlikely, but it was possible. Wellington had little confidence in the Northern Powers, owing to their divergent aims and interests and the jealousies amongst their military commanders. Possibly he foresaw that during the negotiations Napoleon was likely to raise points, such as those relating to maritime trade and the French occupation of Antwerp, not of capital interest to Russia or Prussia, but which the British Government considered of vital importance: that consequently disagreements might lead to concessions by Napoleon, and a separate peace with Russia and Prussia.

This opinion seems to have been fairly general in the allied army. Larpent mentions it,[1] and Sir T. Graham, writing to Wellington on 13th August, says:

---

1. *Larpents Journal,* 2nd July, 1813. "If the armistice produces a Russian and Prussian peace, and we are left to Bonaparte's sole attention, we may see Portugal again in spite of the latest glorious victory."

We shall probably be left, as usual, in the lurch by the allies to whom Bonaparte will make concessions in order to be free to act against Spain. It never seems to have been impressed on the minds of the northern Powers that securing the independence of Spain was one of the severest blows to Bonaparte's overwhelming influence in Europe.[1]

Replying on the same day, Wellington writes:

The allies appear to be well together—but they have not agreed upon the basis. Much less on the peace for which they are entering on negotiations, nor is there in any of the documents sent me [1] the slightest trace of their making common cause with England and Spain by which alone the peace of the world can be secured.[2]

Meanwhile arrangements had been made in London to facilitate the speedy transmission to Wellington of any decision arrived at by the Congress of Prague. Certain code words, each denoting a possible result of the Conference, were decided upon, communicated to Wellington, and a Foreign Office messenger carrying these was sent to Plymouth, where the admiral had orders to have a ship ready to sail on receipt of a message containing any one of these words. News of Austria's declaration of war reached London on 27th August. The corresponding code word "Austrian war" was sent by semaphore telegraph and reached Plymouth at 7 p.m., the messenger sailed at once for Passages in H.M.S. *Gleaner* and the message reached Wellington on or before the 5th Sep-

---

1. Information regarding affairs in Northern Europe generally reached Wellington in the form of copies or precis of the dispatches and reports of commanders and other agents of the Government sent him by the Foreign Office. From the date of these it would appear the papers reached him in from four to six weeks after the originals had been written.
2. It had become known also about this time that Napoleon had been considering the question of making peace with Spain by the restoration of Ferdinand VII as king of Spain.

tember, as on that date he wrote to Lord William Bentinck informing him of the denunciation of the armistice and that hostilities would be renewed on the 16th.

On political as well as military grounds Wellington had decided not to advance immediately; but to secure what he had gained and prepare for a future forward movement.

To do this it was necessary to establish a regular, speedy and as secure as possible system for the supply of the army; not an easy matter owing to the extended position of the army, the increased distances of the sea bases and the difficult intervening country with its indifferent communications. Nearer harbours were very necessary.

Napoleon said that "fortresses in themselves will not arrest an army, but they are an excellent means of retarding, embarrassing, weakening and annoying a victorious; enemy."[1] Now, on or near two of the chief roads leading from Spain into France were the two fortresses of San Sebastian and Pamplona; both had either to be captured or masked if there was to be security on the communications.

It had been Wellington's original intention to besiege them both, but, on reconsideration, he judged his means insufficient for two sieges, and regarding San Sebastian and its harbour as the more important, decided to besiege the place, using Graham's corps for the purpose, and to blockade Pamplona by the Conde de la Bispal's Andalusian Reserve, then moving up from Pancorbo, and Don Carlos's[2] division of the 4th Spanish Army. Another harbour, Passages, was available, as its garrison had surrendered; but situated as it is between San Sebastian and the French frontier, distant only 7 miles, the port could not be a really safe one for the landing of stores and supplies as long as the fortress remained in possession of the French. Though its entrance is narrow between high cliffs and not easy to make in a foul wind, the port is a good one and had to be used.

---

1. *Military Maxims of Napoleon.* XL.
2. General Don Carlos de Espana was a French *emigri* who had taken service in the Spanish army.

In accordance with Wellington's decision not to advance, the following distribution of the allied army was carried out.

Byng's brigade of the 2nd Division, one brigade of the Portuguese Division, and Morillo's Spanish Division held the pass of Roncevaux and the adjacent heights covering the road from St. Jean Pied-de-Port to Pamplona and Tudela, with the 4th Division in support at Linzoain, Campbell's brigade of the Portuguese Division being in the Alduides valley.

The remainder of Hill's Corps held the Maya pass and the Baztan valley, through which passes the road from Bayonne to Pamplona by the Maya and Velate passes. In rear of Hill the 3rd Division was at Olague, whence it could move either towards the 4th Division by Eugui or into the Baztan by the Col de Velate.

The 6th Division was at Santesteban, an important road junction at the south-west corner of the Baztan valley. The light division was on the Santa Barbara heights facing Vera and the Bayonnette mountains. The 7th Division held the pass of Echalar. Longa's Spaniards held the heights on the left bank of the Bidassoa river, his left connecting with the 4th Spanish Army divisions holding the San Marcial heights, Irun and the left bank of the Bidassoa estuary to the sea.[1]

The actual siege work against San Sebastian was allotted to the 5th division and two Portuguese brigades commanded by Generals Wilson and Bradford, while the 1st Division held a position across "the great road" between Renteria and Passages to cover both the siege and the port of Passages and whence it could also support the Spanish divisions holding the line of the Bidassoa.

On the 17th July Wellington established his headquarters at Lesaca. On the same morning the fortified convent of San Bartolome in front of San Sebastian was assaulted and taken. On the 19th the siege batteries were armed, and fire on the fortress was opened the next day.

---

1. A small redoubt near Cap de Higuer, commanding the entrance to the estuary, was held by a party of sailors from Sir George Collier's squadron.

Designed to cover two operations running concurrently, the siege of San Sebastian and the blockade of Pamplona, the front was necessarily a long one. From the Altobiscar heights above Roncevaux to the sea is about 32 miles as the crow flies, but considerably longer if measured along the watershed. Communication along the frontier on the Spanish sides was kept up by Vandeleur's and Long's light cavalry brigades, and the 1ist Hussars, King's German Legion, Fane's brigade and the 4th Portuguese Cavalry were about Monreal and Sanguessa, watching the exits from the Irati and other valleys to the eastward. All the other cavalry brigades were about Pamplona and towards the Ebro.

Within the frontier held by the allied army the passages. over the mountains were many, but then as now, the lines suitable for the advance of a large force were limited to the three roads already mentioned as being covered by the army. These are now fine well-graded roads, but in 1813, with the exception of the coast or "great road," were little more than mule tracks.

CHAPTER 2

Wellington

At this time Wellington was in his forty-fifth year, in good health and at the height of his powers and experience. As a commander in the field, his position was a very strong one. Whilst in the previous years of the war there had been not a few, both in and out of Parliament, who hastened to belittle him as a general, and reckoned him dangerous as a man, now all was different. The campaign of 1813 and the crowning victory of Vitoria had swept away criticism. When Parliament met in November, 1813, the only fault the opposition could find with the Government as regards its conduct of the war, was that it had insufficiently supported Wellington with men, money and supplies. The whole nation was for him.

To the Government he was more than merely the general whom they trusted. He had become their adviser; and no one can study his dispatches and private letters to Ministers without remarking how much they seemed to rely on his judgment, and not on purely military and Peninsular affairs alone. Doing so, they gave him practically a free hand.

With the allied Powers his reputation was very high. Indeed, in some respects his position as a commander can be compared to that of Napoleon. As he himself said to Larpent[1]:

---

1. *Larpent's Journal,* 7th August, 1813.

.... he had great advantages now over every other General. He could do what others dare not attempt; and he had got the confidence of the allied Powers—that he had several of the advantages possessed by Bonaparte, in regard to his freedom of action and power of" risking without being constantly called to account, that Bonaparte was quite free from all inquiry; and that he himself was in fact very much so.

There is, however, another side to the picture. Outside the burden of the actual command of forces composed of three nations, Wellington had to shoulder the load of some serious and troublesome difficulties.

Though the army had recovered itself, its fighting strength had been considerably reduced by the casualties in the Battle of Vitoria and in the fighting in the Pyrenees, and the British Government had not taken advantage of the enthusiasm created by the victory of Vitoria to increase its strength.

Wellington was short of money, as he had been throughout the campaign. The pay of the army was several months in arrears. The Spanish muleteers, who provided the land transport of the army, had not been settled up with for twenty months, the army was in debt in all parts of Spain. Had he the necessary funds when he entered France and been able to pay ready money for such supplies as could be bought there, he knew it would go far towards gaining the confidence of the people; but so far the money was not forthcoming.

He was also in conflict with the Spanish Government as regards his position of Generalissimo of their military forces. With the sanction of the British Government he had accepted this command on the understanding that the Spanish Government agreed to certain conditions which he put to it, and which after discussion that Government accepted on 7th January, 1813, and informed him accordingly. But Wellington soon found that, despite of promises and decrees, the

Spanish Government did not mean to honour the engagements entered into with him, which were being continually
broken, notwithstanding his protests.

The crisis came in July, 1813, after Vitoria, when the Government removed from their commands General Castanos,
Captain General of Galicia and commander of the 4th Spanish Army, and his nephew General Giron, who commanded
the portion of the 4th Army, then serving under Wellington's
personal command, and appointed Generals Lacey and Freyre
to the commands thus rendered vacant, the orders of removal
and appointment being sent direct to the officers concerned.

The removal of Castanos and Giron was not a breach of the
agreement with Wellington, but the appointments of Lacey
and Freyre were distinctly so, as by the agreement no officer
was to be appointed to a command except on Wellington's
recommendation; as was also the sending of the orders direct
to the officers and not through the *Generalissimo*, who had
a Spanish staff attached to his headquarters for the purpose.
Moreover the Spanish Government, to show its malevolence,
refused to give effect to Wellington's recommendations for
the promotion of certain Spanish officers for good service
during the Vitoria Campaign.

Wellington was very hurt; he felt "he had been unworthily
treated by the Spanish Government" and told them so in a
firm but perfectly courteous letter.[1] The reply of the Spanish War Minister brought another factor into the case, for
he informed Wellington that the new Regency, which had
come into power [2] since the signing of the agreement, did not
consider itself bound by that made with its predecessor. This
brought the British Government into the affair, and Wellington was directed to suspend the execution of the order for the
removal of Castanos and Giron "until the further pleasure of
the Spanish Government is signified thereon." But Wellington

---

1. Wellington to O'Donoju Huarte, 2nd July, 1813.
2. On 8th March, 1813.

was not anxious to proceed to extremities, for he knew what dangers such action might produce, and therefore wrote to his brother, telling him to explain[1] to the Regency and the War Minister his exact reasons for the protest he had made, and also to the Minister in conciliatory terms, explaining that his original letter was written on the grounds of the removals of the generals at that particular time, when the army was engaged in active operations against the enemy, and not as a remonstrance against the act as a breach of the agreement with him, nor did he regard the refusal of the Regency to promote the Vitoria officers in the same light. What he did complain of was the appointments of Lacey and Freyre without reference to him, and that the Regency should deny it ever intended to adhere, when it authorized the former War Minister to inform him on the 28th March that it accepted it; that he hoped the Minister would now explain the intention of the Government in language which cannot be misunderstood. He added that he desired to serve the Spanish nation, to whom he was indebted, in every possible way, and would continue to do so at the head of the British and Portuguese armies, whatever the decision of the Regency might be, and that, if he was obliged to resign the command of the Spanish armies, he would do so at the time, and in the manner most convenient to the Government.

The "soft answer" had effect. Wellington's letter apparently gave much satisfaction to the Regency.[2] He was informed that he had the full confidence of the Government, and was to consider himself as exercising the full powers of a *Generalissimo*, but without the title. General Giron was permitted to return to the 4th Army; but the removal of Castaños was

[1] Wellington to Henry Wellesley, Ambassador to the Spanish Government. Lesaca, 24th July, 1813. "One advantage resulting from it (his command) is this, that the army is directed to repel the common enemy, and is kept clear of all interference in the disputes of the day. This would not be the case if the command was in the hands of any person who could feel an interest in these parties."

[2] H. Wellesley to Wellington, 16th August.

insisted on. The War Minister's reply, however, brought no answer to Wellington's request regarding the future status of the agreement. For the moment he accepted the situation without further comment, being aware, as has been mentioned, of the danger; on the 30th August, however, he again wrote to the War Minister giving his reasons why he must insist on the terms of the agreement being adhered to, and that it was necessary the Government should come to an early and final decision on the subject. "Therefore," he said, "in case the Regency should not think it proper to comply with my request, I beg leave hereby to resign the command of the Spanish armies with which the Regency and its Cortes have honoured me."

On the 22nd September the War Minister replied that the resignation was provisionally accepted, pending its being laid before the new Cortes when it assembled, and he was requested to retain the command until further instructions reached him. It is unnecessary to go into further details of the matter, but the result was that he exercised the command, until at the end of the campaign when all the Spanish troops had re-crossed the French frontier, on the 13th June, 1814,. he formally resigned it in a letter to the King of Spain.

Another constant and serious difficulty which confronted Wellington was the inadequate co-operation of the Navy with the Army. Dependent as the army was on sea transport for almost everything it required—reinforcements, munitions, money, clothing and most of its food and forage—it was essential that the transports and store ships conveying them through waters infested by French and American privateers should have adequate protection which the Navy alone could supply.

From the opening of the campaign in 1813, when the need was urgent owing to the opening of a new base at Santander, to the end of the war, the naval force allotted to the protection of the sea routes along the western and northern coasts of Spain was either insufficient or badly applied, to safeguard the sea traffic and to suppress the coasting trade between Bordeaux, Bayonne and St. Jean de Luz. The consequences were serious enough. The ships at Lisbon which were loaded and ready to sail on 12th May, were still there on 19th June, and the military stores and provisions which Wellington expected to find at Santander had not arrived there on 2nd July whereby the refitting of the army and the formation of magazines was grievously delayed. Even whilst the siege of San Sebastian was going on the Navy was unable to prevent almost daily communication between the fortress and St. Jean de Luz and Bayonne, and the French were able to introduce supplies and reinforcements for the garrison; whilst reinforcements for the Portuguese army awaiting embarkation at Lisbon to join the army could not be sent owing to want of transports and of convoy.

Wellington's protests from July, 1813, to January, 1814, were constant and caustic. All, he said, he required, was full and safe communication along the coast of Spain and Portugal from Gibraltar to Passages, and the suppression of the coast traffic on the French Biscay coast. But his protests were unavailing. The Admiralty pleaded insufficient means and the dangers of the Biscay coast. But the plea seems inadequate, battleships were not required; and if the Admiralty had prevented the admirals responsible from "tearing their cruisers to pieces in long and distant excursions"[1]—were they in quest of prize money?—these with a few additions would probably have been fully sufficient to ensure the needed protection. As for the dangers, the mercantile marine had to, and did face them despite many losses. The Admiralty did not rise to the occasion; but the Government as a whole was to blame for not compelling the Admiralty to pay attention to Wellington's reiterated demands for naval protection.

---

1. Lord Melville, First Lord of Admiralty to Wellington, 25th July, 1813. "I believe it will be found that Admiral Martin (at Lisbon) had not less than twelve vessels applicable to the sole purpose of protecting the coast from Cape St. Vincent to Cape Finisterre if his cruisers had not been tearing themselves to pieces in long and distant excursions."

CHAPTER 3

Soult & the French Army

With the exception of the troops under General Foy, the army which entered France after its retreat from Vitoria was in a state of disorganization and confusion. It had lost almost all its *materiel* and transport, officers and men had nothing but what they stood up in. Units and brigades had become mixed up; and the districts adjoining the frontier were thronged with stragglers who looted the houses and flocks of the country people. The positions of the various corps were unknown to general headquarters and owing to this and the loss of transport, the supply system broke down completely and the soldiers were almost starving.

Major Baltazar, an A.D.C. of the Minister of War, sent to Bayonne to obtain details of the battle and the state of the army, described the latter as being in a state of anarchy,[1] adding that what the situation required was "an army and a general."

When Napoleon recalled Marshal Soult from Spain he apparently foresaw that events there might oblige him to send Soult back to Spain, so he kept him close at hand in a nominal position at his headquarters. The news of the battle of Vitoria reached the Emperor at Dresden on the 1st July. He at once issued a decree appointing Soult as Commander-in-Chief in Spain and Lieutenant of the Emperor.

---

1. Baltazar to Guerre, 6th July, 1813.

Soult was directed to leave Dresden the same day and proceed to Bayonne, not remaining in Paris more than twelve hours. On the 5th July Napoleon wrote to the Count de Cassac, Minister of War administrations.[1]

I have given the Duke of Dalmatia full authority to reorganize the army. I have forbidden the King of Spain to interfere in my affairs, and I suppose the Duke of Dalmatia will also cause Marshal Jourdan (King Joseph's chief of the staff) to withdraw from the army. Unless the losses are much greater than I know at present, I hope that 100,000 men will soon be assembled on the Bidassoa and before the pass of Jaca (Somport) and that, as soon as you can provide him with artillery and transport, the Duke of Dalmatia will advance to relieve Pamplona and drive the English beyond the Ebro.

Soult arrived at Bayonne on the 12th July and at once proceeded to reorganize the army, which until his arrival had retained the organization in which it had fought at Vitoria, namely the armies of the north, centre, south, and of Portugal. But when giving it a new commander, Napoleon decided that these now out-of-date commands should cease to exist. There was to be one army only, that of Spain, organized on a divisional basis: there were to be no *corps d'armee,* but he left it to Soult to place such number of divisions as he considered suitable under each of the Lieutenant-Generals,[2] the former army commanders, the strength of the divisions to be about 6,000.

There were then fourteen divisions in the four armies. Four were broken up and distributed amongst the remainder, which were numbered from one to nine, the tenth being designated the Reserve Division, in which were incorporated all the foreign troops serving in the army. Namely one brigade

---

1. *Correspondance de Napoleon I.* Dresden, 5th July, 1813. No. 20229.
2. The ages of the Lieutenant-Generals were: Reille, 38; Clausel, 41; and D'Erlon, 46 years. Wellington and Soult were of the same age, 44 years.

of Germans, one of Italians and one of Spaniards, to which was added a strong brigade of six French battalions. Each of the other divisions consisted of two brigades, the number of battalions in which varied from three to five.

These divisions were grouped in three bodies.

The right wing, commanded by Lieutenant-General Count Reille: composed of the 1st Division, General Foy; 7th Division, General Maucune; 9th Division, General Lamartiniere.

The centre, Lieutenant-General Count d'Erlon: 2nd Division, General Darmagnac; 3rd Division, General Abbé; 6th Division, General Maransin.

Left wing, Lieutenant-General Baron Clausel: 4th Division, General Conroux; 5th Division, General Vaudermaesen; 8th Division, General Taupin; Reserve Division, General Villatte.

Four cavalry divisions had been recalled by the Emperor, and two only now remained with the army of Spain. Treilhard's dragoon division of two brigades, and a mixed division of three brigades under P. Soult, a brother of the Marshal.[1]

Sixty-two guns had reached Bayonne with the convoy sent from Vitoria on the morning of the battle. These formed the nucleus of the re-armament of the artillery. Other guns and stores were received from Rochefort, Bordeaux and Toulouse, and the Bayonne arsenal provided 400 ammunition wagons.

Eventually the army was equipped with 149 field and mountain guns and howitzers; these were divided as follows:—to each infantry division a battery of eight pieces, six guns and two howitzers; to each cavalry division a horse battery of six pieces; to the Reserve Division four batteries of eight pieces. Each wing and the centre had also a mountain battery of six guns. In the artillery park there was a reserve of 21 guns. The field guns were 12- and 8-pounders, the mountain guns 4-pounders.

On the 16th July the strength of the reorganized army, officers and men present, and fit for duty was 70,369 in-

---

1. From this division one light cavalry regiment was attached to each of the Lieutenant-General's commands.

fantry, 7,081 cavalry, Troops *hors de ligne* artillery, its train and artificers, sappers, gendarmerie, etc., 14,938, a total of 92,388, which does not include the garrisons of Bayonne, San Sebastian and Pamplona; at Bayonne 5,950 conscripts were under training. The number of men sick, wounded and on command was 16,184, making with the recruits a grand total of 114,522.

But reorganization and new equipment was not all the army needed. Its moral and discipline had slackened severely since Vitoria; to re-establish both was a primary necessity, and Soult set about doing so sternly. A permanent Court Martial was established, the numerous soldiers out of the ranks under various pretexts were hunted out and sent back to their regiments. The camps were cleared of the crowds of hangers-on, including many Spanish women, who had attached themselves to the army before and during the retreat. A month's pay was issued to the army; but by the Emperor's orders, the officers of all ranks ceased to receive any of the allowances hitherto given in Spain.[1]

There is no doubt that Soult's presence and his vigorous efforts had a good effect on the army. Baltazar, whose report on 6th July has been quoted, was on the 23rd able to report to the Minister of War as follows—*"J'ai vu presque toute l'armee; il est difficile d'imaginer de plus ' belles troupes."*[2]

But it cannot be said that the nomination of Soult to the chief command was well received throughout all ranks of the army. With the exception of a few generals and other officers who had served with him in Spain, and hoped to profit thereby, the army would have preferred Marshal Suchet, then commanding the armies of Catalonia and Aragon.

Nicolas Jean Soult, Marshal of France since 1804 and Duke of Dalmatia, was, like Wellington, then in his forty-fourth year.

---

1. *Correspondence de Napoleon,* No. 20236, Dresden, 6th July.
2. Baltazar to Guerre, Bayonne, 23rd July, 1813, and Soult to Guerre, 19th July. "The army has regained confidence, the soldiers speak of the last reverse only to manifest the resolution to avenge it in a brilliant manner."

A big man with a large head, very marked features and piercing eyes, his manners were rough and surly and his treatment of his subordinates often harsh and vindictive. He was essentially a selfish man whose word could not be relied on, and he had a great greed for money.

Nevertheless, Soult was endowed with great organizing abilities, great powers of work and large experience. As a strategist his views were large and vigorous; as a leader in the field, however, he lacked confidence, hesitated to give orders or change his plan when things were not going as he had expected, and he had not that eye for seeing at once the decisive moment of an engagement nor that faculty for judging in action the state of the enemy's moral which so distinguished his Emperor and his present opponent.

On the 19th July, the army of Spain was distributed as follows—

The right wing under Reille held the right bank of the Bidassoa from the sea to the Bayonnette mountain. The centre, D'Erlon, Abbé and Maransin's divisions about Ainhoa, with outposts at Zugaramurdi and Urdax. Darmagnac's division about Espelette.

Left wing. Clausel at St. Jean Pied-de-Port with Couroux's division at St. Etienne de Baigorry with detachments watching the passes into the Baztan valley. Soult's headquarters were at Bayonne.

The instructions Soult had received from the Emperor were to take, without delay, measures to save San Sebastian, Pamplona and Pancorbo (the latter had surrendered on the 1st July), to take the offensive for that purpose and to re-enter Spain as speedily as possible.[1] Having reorganized and re-equipped the army, he had now to decide how it should be employed, to relieve San Sebastian or Pamplona? The de-

1. Instruction addressee a M. le Marechal Duc de Dalmatie, 7th July, 1813. Napoleon recognized that when he gave verbal orders to Soult and issued his decree of 1st July, he really knew very little of what had happened. Napoleon to Lacuce. *Corr.*, No. 20229.

cision could not be delayed, for the Emperor was impatient and ardently desired a success in Spain with which to stifle the effect of Vitoria, and this he thought he could do, if his delegate to the Congress of Prague could announce the relief of Pamplona by Soult.

The latter hesitated for some time, but having been assured by the aide-de-camp of General Rey, who had come to his headquarters on 18th July, that San Sebastian could hold out for more than fifteen days, Soult decided to attempt the relief of Pamplona. His plan was briefly as follows—

To use for his advance the two roads which led from the centre and left of the line he held, namely that from Ainhoa by the passes of Maya and Velate to Pamplona, and that from St. Jean Pied-de-Port by Roncevaux to Pamplona, the main advance being made by the latter route with six divisions composed of Reille's right wing and Clausel's divisions already at St. Jean Pied-de-Port, whilst D'Erlon with his three divisions advanced against the Maya position held by Hill's corps; the positions held by Reille's corps being taken up by Villatte's reserve division.

The concentration of Reille's corps commenced on the 20th July; it was delayed by the bad state of the country roads used, owing to the heavy rain which fell on the 19th and 20th, but was completed by the evening of the 23rd; the two cavalry divisions and the artillery, 66 guns, having arrived on the 22nd. On the 23rd Soult issued his order for the general advance which was to take place at 4 a.m. on the 25th, and on that day he wrote as follows to the War Minister:

I have just issued the last order of movement to attack the enemy—I propose also to manoeuvre so as to threaten the enemy's communication with Tolosa and Vitoria and so compel him to quickly retire towards the Ebro. The result of this movement ought also to relieve San Sebastian, and, unless I am mistaken in my hope, ought to compromise several of his corps.

The first paragraph of the order referred to states that "during the 23rd and 24th an issue of four days' ration shall be made to all the troops." But the supply arrangements were all out of joint. Reille's troops were to have received several days' supply of biscuits on starting for the concentration, but biscuits were not forthcoming, so flour, which had to be carried in the men's haversacks, was issued instead, only to become sodden owing to the rain. Nor were supply measures any better at St. Jean Pied-de-Port where confusion reigned. Flour and grain were insufficient for the needs of the assembled troops, the bakeries could not turn out the bread and biscuits required, and matters came to such a pass that the oxen required to drag the guns up the pass had to be guarded against the hungry soldiers as well as the houses of the villagers, whose menfolk were away in the mountains doing their duty as national guards. It is doubtful if even the most lucky units in the army received more than two days' rations; those of D'Erlon corps on the 25th had nothing more than the rations for the day.[1]

Nevertheless on the 25th the advance took place. On the same day the assault on San Sebastian was made and failed, and Wellington, hearing late in the day of the French movements, ordered Graham to withdraw the armament from the siege batteries and blockade the place only.

It would be out of place here to go into any detail of the almost continuous fighting in the mountains which followed Soult's advance on the 25th July. It will suffice to state that after the nine days' struggle, Soult's expedition, which aimed at relieving both fortresses and driving the allies beyond the Ebro, ended in failure. On the night of the 2nd August the French army was back in France. The army indeed had been saved, but at a cost of 13,163 officers and men killed, wounded and prisoners, and its moral was gone. The troops had no longer confidence in themselves or in their leader. Major Baltazar, writing to the War Minister, said:

1.Vidal de la Blache *L'Evacuation de L'Espagne,* I.

I cannot conceal from your Excellency that the result of this unfortunate campaign has had a most mischievous effect on the spirit of the army in general, and the state of affairs has become even more unfortunate than after the retreat in June.[1]

The heavy losses in certain of the French divisions necessitated their reconstruction. When this had been done the army took up practically the same line as before the advance, but the distribution of the troops along it was altered. As before Reille's corps, less Foy's division which was detached on the extreme left,[2] was on the right, Maucune's division holding from the sea to Biriatou, Larmartiniere the Mandale and the Bayonnette mountain above Vera. Villatte's reserve division about Serres and Ascain.

In the centre Clausel had Conroux's and Vandermaesen's divisions encamped to the south of Sare holding the Sta. Barbe and Grenada redoubts, with posts on the tracks to Vera and Echalar, and also on the slopes of the Rhune mountain which fall towards Olhain. Taupin's division was placed on the high ground north of Sare about the Louis XIV redoubt.[3]

On Clausel's left Darmagnac's and Maransin's divisions of D'Erlon's corps were on the high ground to the north of Ainhoa with their left on the Mondarrain mountain. Abbé's division to the north of Urdax with a post in that village and also in Zugaramurdi.

Foy's division was at St. Jean Pied-de-Port with posts towards Roncevaux and in the Baigorry valley. The defence of the high valleys to the east of Roncevaux was entrusted to the local national guards, and Paris's brigade was placed between St. Palais and St. Jean to cover the roads to St. Palais and Mauleon.

---

1. Baltazar to Guerre, Bayonne, 2nd August, 1813.
2. During the retreat after the fight at Sorauren on 30th July, Foy's division, accompanied by a large number of stragglers of other divisions, had become separated from the rest of the army, and finally arrived at Cambo on the Nive.
3. There were two redoubts of this name, the above at point 232 on French map to N.E. of Sare, the other on hill Louis XIV above Behobie.

CHAPTER 4

Holding the Frontier

On 1st August, the last day but one of the French retreat from Sorauren, Wellington had it in his mind to follow the French and cross the frontier. He ordered Graham to get up the pontoon train, artillery and cavalry and make all arrangements for crossing the Bidassoa, whilst still keeping up the blockade of San Sebastian. As soon, however, as he received full details of the state of the army and its casualties, he decided to postpone a further advance, and to replace the army in its former positions along the frontier.

Writing on the 8th August to the Secretary of State he said:

.... an army which has made such marches and fought such battles, as that under my command has, is necessarily much deteriorated. Independently of the actual loss of numbers by death, wounds and sickness, many men and officers are out of the ranks for various causes.[1] The equipment of the army, its ammunition, the soldiers' shoes, etc., require renewal, magazines for the new operations require to be collected and formed, and many arrangements made without which the army could not exist for a day. . . .

Then observe, that this new operation is only the invasion of France, in which country everybody is a soldier, where

---

1. There was no medical corps in those days. To tend the sick and wounded in hospitals and convalescent depots, men from the ranks had to be employed.

the whole population is armed and organized, under persons, not, as in other countries inexperienced in arms, but men who, in the course of the last 2 5 years in which France has been engaged in war with all Europe, must, the majority of them at least, have served somewhere.

I entertain no doubt I could enter France to-morrow and establish the army on the Adour, but I could go no further certainly. If peace is made by the Powers of the North, I must necessarily withdraw into Spain, and the retreat however short would be difficult owing to the hostility and warlike disposition of the inhabitants particularly of this part of the country and the military direction they would receive from the gentry their leaders. To this add, that the difficulty of all that must be done to set the army to rights, after its late severe battles and victories will be much increased by its removal into France at too early a period.

So far for the immediate invasion of France, which, from what I have seen of the state of the negotiations in the north of Europe, I have determined to consider only in reference to the convenience of my own operations.

Having thus decided against an immediate advance, orders were issued on 5th August for the reoccupation by the army of the line held on 25th July. But a review of the operations from that date to 2nd August discloses two main weaknesses in the original distribution. The first, the insufficient strength of the allied forces holding the extreme right about Roncevaux, the Maya ridge and the Baztan valley. The second, the general neglect all along the line to increase the defensive strength of the positions held by entrenchments.

The new distribution ordered shows that the lesson had been learnt. The command on the right was given to Sir R. Hill with an increased force, namely the whole 2nd Division, the Portuguese Division, Morillo's Spanish Division and the 13th Light Dragoons. With this force he was to hold the passes about Roncevaux and in the Alduides valley, where his corps was to be responsible for the protection of the right flank of the troops holding the Maya ridge and the Baztan valley.

The defence of the Maya pass and the Baztan valley was entrusted to the 3rd and 6th Divisions and 14th Light Dragoons under Sir T. Picton. The 6th Division was to occupy the Maya pass and its neighbourhood, with the 3rd in support at Ariscun, which division was also to watch the passes which communicate with the Alduides valley, and keep touch with Hill's corps. Both Hill and Picton were reminded how important the prompt communication of intelligence was in the present situation of the army, and that a standing system of cavalry letter parties was *to* be established for the passing of information and orders to the right and left and also to the rear by Almandoz and Lanz. Picton was also informed that Wellington considered it essential that the division holding the Maya ridge should have a piquet in the village of Urdax at the foot of the hill on the French side.

On the left of the 6th Division, the 7th held the ridge which, springing from the Atchuria mountain, runs north-eastwards towards the village of Ainhoa.

The Andalusian Reserve occupied Echalar and its pass, and the 4th Division Lesaca, where general headquarters were established.

The Light Division held the Santa Barbara heights over-looking Vera. On its left Longa's Spanish Division watched the left bank of the Bidassoa from the Zalain of Vera to the ford of Enderlazza.

The 3rd, 4th and 5th Divisions with part of the 7th[1] Division of the 4th Spanish Army held the heights of San Marcial, the towns of Irun and Fuenterabia and the estuary of the Bidassoa to the sea. In support was the 1st British Division and

1 The remainder of this division was blockading Santona.

Vandeleur's cavalry brigade, whilst further to the rear was the San Sebastian siege corps, consisting of the 5th Division and Wilson's and Bradford's Portuguese brigades.

Carlos de Espana's division of the 4th Army with one division of the Andalusian Reserve[1] was blockading Pamplona. As no danger threatened in Aragon, Mina, less his detachment blockading Jaca, was brought up first to Tudela and then to Sanguesa.

The cavalry, with the exception of the two light brigades employed at the front, remained about Pamplona and towards the Ebro.

When the divisions reached their positions, the work of strengthening the ground commenced. About Roncevaux and the Lindux redoubts, blockhouses and trenches commanding the approaches were thrown up.[2] A soldier writes:[3] "Our labour was incessant, working like galley-slaves building batteries and blockhouses," and so it went on all along the line. On the extreme left more elaborate works were planned after Wellington had made a personal inspection of the whole ground.

He designed to have three lines of defence between the Bidassoa and Passages.[4] The first ran from the Andarra valley along the San Marcial heights; this line, he considered, required no works beyond trenches, breastworks and abattis; but in rear of its extreme right were to be two strong redoubts, and on its left a closed battery was to be built immediately above the broken bridge of Behobie to prevent the enemy repairing it

---

1. This division was relieved on 17th September by a division of the 3rd Spanish Army, which Wellington had brought up to Tudela, and rejoined its corps at Echalar.

2. Hope, *Military Memoirs,* p. 344. Engineer officers had been sent to all divisions to assist in strengthening the positions held.

3. *Journal of a Soldier. Memorials of the late War,* p. 121. Some of these redoubts and trenches remain to the present day; they appear well sited.

4. Wellington to Colonel Fletcher, C.R.E., and to Graham, 15th August: "You may depend upon it that, whatever we do elsewhere, we cannot make the position between Oyarzun and the Bidassoa too strong. Meanwhile it is desirable that no time should be lost in commencing the works you propose. The second line is, if possible, more important than the first, which is not very easily held without a strong second line."

or laying a pontoon bridge near it. The second line was to be on a ridge running down from the Crown Mountain (Pena de Haya) towards the main road on which there were to be several works. The first and second lines were continued in one line to the sea by the little town of Irun put in a state of defence with a redoubt about half a mile in rear of it and thence to the mouth of the estuary by eight redoubts connected by breastworks and trenches. The third line was on the high ground connecting the lower slopes of the Haya with those of the Jaizquibel mountain in front of Oyarzun, which immediately covered the siege operations at San Sebastian.

There was greater delay in resuming active siege operations than Wellington had expected, because a new siege train, ordered from England some time previously, had not arrived, and most of the old guns, which had been removed from the batteries and embarked on transports when Soult advanced on the 25th July, were, on examination after disembarkation on 5th August, found to be unfit for further use.[1]

On 19th August transports arrived with a division of 28 new guns; a second of 27 guns was followed on the 23rd by a third of 28 guns, and on the 26th August fire on the fortress was resumed.

Meanwhile the allied troops were busy strengthening their positions, their needs in equipment and ammunition were being supplied, and Wellington awaited the fall of San Sebastian and further news regarding the negotiations between the Powers in the north.

On the 11th August Lord Bathurst forwarded to him extracts from a scheme for an allied advance into France which a French *emigre* officer[2] had submitted to the Foreign Office because it contained some local information regarding places

---

1. The number of rounds fired during the first siege "had not only caused the metal to droop at the muzzle, but had so enlarged the vents that few of (hem were at all serviceable." Henegan (Chief Officer of the Field Train), *Campaigning in the Peninsula.*
2. Probably General Dumouriez.

in Southern France which the Minister thought might be useful. In reply Wellington wrote as follows:

> I have received your letter with General ——'s scheme. It is like all those I have received from French officers, and might answer well enough if I could afford, or the British Government or Nation would allow of my being as prodigal of men as every French general is. They forget, however, that we have but one army, that the same men who fought at Vimiero and Talavera fought the other day at Sorauren, and that, if I am to preserve the army, I must proceed with caution. Indeed, this becomes doubly necessary as I see that notwithstanding the fondness of the British nation for the sport, they began to cry out the other day at the loss of 300 to 400 men in the unsuccessful assault of San Sebastian and of the men in the affair at the Maya .... Your Lordship may depend upon it that I am by no means tired of success, and that I shall do everything in my power to draw the attention of the enemy to this quarter as soon as I shall know that hostilities are really renewed in Germany.[1]

There is no doubt that at this time Wellington was anxious about the strength of his army, especially as regards its backbone, the British infantry. Including the losses at the Battle of Vitoria the total casualties in action up to the 3rd August had been 720 officers and 12,260 other ranks, of whom 107 officers and 2,498 other ranks had been killed or were missing, and practically the whole loss had been in the infantry.

On the 21st June, 1813, at Vitoria the British and Portuguese infantry fighting strength present under arms was: British, 1,681 officers, 38,564 other ranks; Portuguese, 983 officers and 25,904 other ranks; total, 2,664 officers and 64,468 other ranks.[2]

---

1. Wellington to Bathurst, Lesaca, 23rd August, 1813.
2. See Appendix D. In these figures taken from weekly and monthly states, the strength of the 1st Guards Brigade of 1st Division are not included as the brigade had been left at Oporto owing to sickness and did not rejoin the army until 18th August. Nor are included a British battalion at Lisbon, the Wagon Train, and men prisoners of war and missing still on the strength of units.

On the 16th July, before the fighting in the Pyrenees, the infantry fighting strength (exclusive of officers) was: British, 32,152; Portuguese, 23,243; total 55,395.

On the 8th August, after the fighting, the figures were: British, 26,570; Portuguese, 20,402; total, 46,972; giving a total decrease of 17,496 men, and the number of sick and wounded infantry had risen to 22,661.

Further losses[1] must necessarily be expected before San Sebastian could be taken, and there was always the possibility of another French attack.

The allied numerical superiority now consisted entirely in the Spanish troops with the army. Troops which, as Wellington said, "lacked everything necessary to maintain an army in the field," and whom he dreaded to take into France lest their pillage and ill-treatment of the inhabitants should create a general rising in the Basque country. The situation at the beginning of August was an anxious one and it probably influenced Wellington's decision against an immediate advance into France.

Fortunately about this time the wounded at Vitoria were rejoining their regiments in considerable numbers. Writing on nth August, Wellington said: "I believe in the course of this week we shall get up to their regiments 1,500 British and 2,000 Portuguese." On the 25th he was able to report that during the preceding week 500 British and about 1,500 Portuguese had rejoined from the hospitals, and that every day some men were coming up.

"The troops," he said, "continue remarkably healthy, there is, indeed, no sickness amongst them."[2]

---

1. The total casualties during the fighting in the Pyrenees and the unsuccessful attack on San Sebastian on 25th July were 8,334. Writing to Bathurst on 18th August Wellington said: "Our loss is distressing as having fallen a good deal on Hill's corps. The number of British troops there has become too small in proportion to foreigners." Unfortunately, too, desertion at this time was very rife, and by no means confined to the foreign troops.
2. Wellington to Bathurst/25th August, 1813.

Reinforcements were also arriving. On the 18th August the 1st Guards brigade from Oporto rejoined the 1st Division. About the same time three regiments from England, the 76th, 2/84th and 85th, strength 112 officers and 1,817 men, also arrived. These were formed into a brigade under Lord Aylmer.[1] By the 25th August about 800 men in drafts from England had also joined,[2] making a total increase of over 4,000 infantry, so that with the recovered men from convalescent depots and hospitals, Wellington on that date was able to report that he "did not doubt that we are now as strong as we were on the 25th of last (July) month."

During September reinforcements consisting of the 2/62nd Regiment and drafts arrived.[3] With these and recovered men the infantry strength at the beginning of October was raised to British, 34,257; Portuguese, 22,247; total 56,504.

---

1. Wellington to Hope, 18th October, 1813. "It was to nurse the newly arrived troops that I formed Lord Aylmer's brigade."
2. Owing to the absence of a censorship and the indiscretions of newspaper editors the French War Office was well informed of the movements of troops from England. In the Archives de Guerre at Paris amongst the documents received at the Ministry on 17th July, 1813, is the following extract from a London newspaper. The *Star* of 12th July: "Detachments of 27th, 71st, 79th and 92nd regiments left Glasgow last Thursday for Leith, where they embark for Spain."
3. Batty, *Campaign of Western Pyrenees*. "On 30th September fifteen sail of transports entered the harbour of Passages with a reinforcement of 700 men of the foot guards."

CHAPTER 5

Soult Prepares

The French army, when it re-entered France on the 2nd August, was again in a state of considerable disorganization. Its losses had been very heavy—13,163 officers and men—in some of the divisions these had been so great that to equalize the strength units had to be transferred from the less hardly hit divisions.

Some regiments had no more than four officers.[1] Many men were out of the ranks; about 7,500 stragglers had followed the retreat of Foy's division from Sorauren towards St. Jean Pied-de-Port; hungry, exhausted men only kept alive by the food given to them by the inhabitants, or plundered from the latter.

The supply system of the army had again broken down. Half the horses of the artillery had to be taken to assist in the distribution of food, and Soult had been obliged to send all his cavalry, except four squadrons, far to the rear, owing to lack of forage.

Under the circumstances it is not surprising that Soult felt disinclined to attempt another offensive. But the Emperor's orders still stood; and the War Minister had lately told him that as his dispatches gave no indication of how "he proposed to arrest the enemy's progress against the fortresses, His Maj-

---

1. Eight per cent, of the officers of the French divisions were killed in action, 22½ per cent, of the remainder wounded or prisoners of war. In a letter to the War Minister, 1st September, 1813, Soult attributes the heavy limn to the superior marksmanship of the allied light troops.

esty will be astonished to receive the news of your return to the frontier without any details of your plans regarding the besieged places."[1] A request to the Minister for reinforcements, and that the Emperor should be asked for further instructions, drew no reply from the latter, and the Minister's answer was to repeat Napoleon's original instructions, saying that he could neither add to them nor to Soult's means.[2]

So further efforts to relieve Pamplona and San Sebastian had to be made. Both were blockaded; and it must have been evident to Soult that the siege of the latter would probably be speedily renewed. He appears to have been at this time in a very wavering state of mind. Before him were his Emperor's orders; the dangers of an attack on a strong position with a twice-beaten army, the facts, which he must by now have realized, that this army had little confidence in itself or in its Commander, and that the public feeling was depressed owing to his failure to relieve Pamplona.

Soult now bethought him of enlisting the aid of Marshal Suchet[3] commanding the armies of Aragon and Catalonia, in another attempt to relieve Pamplona. His plan, as outlined in a letter to Suchet on 10th August, was that I the latter should advance with all his available troops towards Zaragoza, so as to cover the communication by Jaca between his army and that of Soult, and then manoeuvre in the direction of the army of

---

1. Paper without date in the Archives de Guerre at Paris. The Minister was above all things desirous to get the army out of France as soon as possible so that its pay and upkeep should not fall on French funds.
2. Guerre to Soult, Paris, 9th August, 1813.
3. Though Soult by the Emperor's decree had been appointed his Lieutenant in Spain, this did not give him command over Suchet, because the armies of Aragon and Catalonia were under the direct orders of Napoleon and were never under King Joseph. When the War Minister saw the terms of Soult's appointment, he wrote to the Emperor asking if no reference to Suchet's command was an oversight, but Napoleon gave no reply. The two Marshals had been on bad terms for some years. Soult was jealous of Suchet, and the latter had never forgiven Soult for being the cause of a severe reprimand he had received from Napoleon in 1810.

Spain threatening the allied communications with the Ebro and Spain.[1] Such a move would, he considered, oblige Wellington to detach a considerable force to meet it, thereby weakening his hold on his present line, and so give Soult an opportunity to pierce it and join hands with Suchet when Pamplona might be relieved. "I shall," he said, "be ready to attack as soon as I know you have advanced." This letter did not reach Suchet until the 21st August. His reply reached Soult on the 2nd September. He said that Soult was evidently unaware of the feeble strength of his command, weakened as it was by having to provide so many garrisons and by a large number of sick; that the armies of Aragon and Catalonia between them could not furnish a force of more than from 16,000 to 17,000 men; that the allied troops in front of him had been reinforced by General Hill's troops and la Bispal's Spaniards.[2] He considered Soult's proposal most dangerous and likely to result in another Baylen. Though Soult continued the correspondence for several months, nothing came of it.

But for Soult time was precious if he was to make a further effort to carry out his orders before it was too late. From the date of its investment he had had no communication with Pamplona; the only information he had as to its state was what he had received from Clausel, who had been there in June, which was that there was then sufficient supplies in the fortress for the garrison up to the 25th September, and that it would probably be able to hold out a little longer.

As regards Pamplona, therefore, there seemed no immediate urgency. But it was not so in the case of San Sebastian. From General Rey's reports Soult knew that the allies were preparing to renew the siege, and that, if, the place was to be

---

1. It will be remembered that Wellington's chief object in the employment of the Anglo-Sicilian force and Spanish troops in the north-eastern provinces of Spain was to prevent any combination by Suchet with the main French armies.

2. Here, of course, he was quite mistaken. Probably a rumour put about by Wellington's agents, which it suited Suchet to use.

relieved, he must have a plan of action ready. He determined, therefore, to attack the allied left wing, so as to gain possession of the great road from Bayonne by Irun to Tolosa.

Briefly his plan was that Reille's corps should cross the Bidassoa between Behobie and Biriatou, seize the San Marcial heights, gain the main road and advance by it to Oyarzun, whilst Clausel, with four divisions, was to descend from the Bayonnette, cross the Bidassoa by fords at Enderlaza and Zalain, ascend the Haya mountain, gain touch with Reille's corps, and then descend by its southern slopes on Oyarzun. D'Erlon's corps was to hold its position about Ainhoa, but if the allied troops holding the Maya and Echalar passes moved to join the left wing D'Erlon was to follow them. If the preliminary movements were successful, Soult counted on being able to reunite his columns and then attack the Oyarzun position covering the siege. This gained, the road to Passages and San Sebastian would be open.

This plan Soult submitted to the War Minister with a request that he would submit it to the Emperor, "whose orders I hope to receive before it is put into operation."[1] The Minister approved of the plan; but Napoleon sent no answer.

Soult probably had his doubts as to the chances of success—his army certainly had. Very irresolute, he kept putting off action from day to day in the hope of receiving the Emperor's decision which would absolve him from responsibility. But at length Rey's reports and one from Clausel that the assault was fixed for the 30th obliged him to act, and orders were issued for the advance to be made on the morning of the 30th. Owing, however, to delay in the issue of rations, and the bridge equipment not being ready, the date was altered to 31st. The concentration movements in the French army towards its right had not escaped notice, and Wellington "had every reason to believe that they would make an attempt to relieve the place."[2] To meet this

---

1. Soult to Guerre, Ascain, 17th August, 1813.
2. Wellington to Bathurst, Lesaca, 2nd September, 1813.

he placed the 1st Division and Aylmer's brigade in rear of the left of Freyre's[1] three Spanish divisions holding the San Marcial heights. Longa's division was on the slopes of the Haya in rear of their right. To give further support to this flank the two British brigades of the 4th Division at Lesaca were moved on the 30th August up the mountain to the convent of San Antonio, leaving the Portuguese brigade to hold the high ground between that point and the Bidassoa below Vera. Inglis's brigade of the 7th Division from the pass of Echalar replaced the 4th Division at Lesaca. The 6th and 7th Divisions and Giron's Spanish corps were ordered to demonstrate against the enemy's posts in front of the passes of Maya, Zugaramurdi, and Echalar. Hill at Roncevaux was also told to give, if possible, "the enemy a little alert in your neighbourhood."[2]

Early in the morning of the 31st Reille, with Maucune's and Lamartiniere's divisions, crossed the Bidassoa by fords below the Louis XIV hill and Biriatou, covered by artillery fire from the heights on the right bank. These divisions made "a desperate attack on the whole front held by Freyre's three divisions on the San Marcial heights."[3] Before the assailants reached the summit, the Spaniards charged with much gallantry and drove the attackers in great confusion to the river.

About noon Soult reinforced Reille with part of Villatte's division, and then launched another attack; though the French right gained the summit, this attack met with no greater success than the first: for Wellington, refusing the reinforcement the Spanish desired, ordered another charge. Then the Spaniards, "shouting aloud, dashed their adversaries with such vio-

---

1. Lieut-General Freyre had taken over command of the 4th Army, Giron having been removed from his command by order of the Spanish Minister of War without reference to Wellington, who transferred him to that of the Andalusian Reserve *vice* La Bispal on sick leave owing to wounds.
2. Murray to Hill, Lesaca, 30th August, 1813.
3. Wellington to Bathurst, Lesaca, 2nd September, 1813.

lence that many were driven into the river, and some of the pontoon boats coming to their assistance (the tide now being up) were overloaded and sank."[1]

The conduct of the Spaniards, said Wellington in his dispatch, "was equal to any troops I have seen engaged." Reille's defeated divisions were not rallied on the right bank until several hours later.

Meanwhile, Clausel, leaving Maransin's division on the heights above Vera to contain the Light Division on the Santa Barbara, crossed the Bidassoa by the fords about Zalain and moved up the slopes, which descend in this direction from the Haya mountain, driving back the Portuguese brigade of the 4th Division. Wellington sent Inglis's brigade from Lesaca to its assistance; but the French were too strong, and both brigades fell slowly back to a position below the convent of San Antonio.

About noon Clausel stopped the advance of his main columns, considering it was "not possible or prudent" to advance further until he knew that Reille had gained possession of the San Marcial heights; his advanced troops keeping up a skirmishing action against Inglis's brigades. Now he also began to feel anxious about his left flank and his retreat, for Kempt's brigade of the Light Division had been moved to Lesaca, being replaced on Santa Barbara by some of Giron's troops; and he reported his situation and views to Soult.

The demonstrations along the right of the line, ordered, by Wellington, had been going on since early morning. Giron attacked Couroux's outposts in front of Sare, and the 7th Division those about Zugaramurdi, the Portuguese brigade of the 6th Division attacked the brigade of Abbé's division holding Urdax, and fighting went on all the morning until noon when the French retired and Douglas seized and burnt their camp. Abbé then concentrated his division about Ainhoa. About this time the remainder of the 6th Division

---

1. Napier. "As the tide ascends as far as Biriatou, the fords are impassable at high water."

showed itself on the Maya heights as if moving towards the Mondarrain mountain. When this was reported to D'Erlon, he came to the conclusion that Wellington was about to turn the left of the French line and interpose between it and Bayonne so as to force Soult to retire, and reported accordingly. The fear was groundless, but, according to Soult's dispatch to the War Minister, this report and that of Clausel decided him to refrain from making another attack on St. Marcial and to withdraw his whole army across the Bidassoa.[1]

Between 3 and 4 p.m. an exceedingly heavy storm of rain, wind, and thunder burst over the Haya mountain, and to a great extent put a stop to the fighting. At 5 p.m. Clausel was ordered to re-cross the river and move his three divisions towards Ascain and Serres, to which latter place Foy with some cavalry had already been sent as a support to D'Erlon.

Owing to the heavy rain and the narrowness and steepness of the rocky sides of the valley, when Clausel arrived at the river-bank he found it in flood and rising rapidly. Two or three brigades only were able to cross; for the remainder of the three divisions the only possible means of crossing was by the bridge of Vera.

On the morning of the 31st August when the French advanced they sent some troops to seize the bridge, but "were repulsed in good style by two rifle companies."[2]

> The uncertain result of the operations had rendered it inexpedient to destroy the bridge; but to secure the brigade of the Light Division on the Santa Barbara from sudden attack during the night, the bridge was I partially blocked up with casks filled with stones, leaving only a narrow passage for a man: and a fortified house commanding it occupied by a company of the 95th Rifles.[3]

---

1. Vidalde la Blache, says: "All these statements do not agree with the facts. Clausel was left isolated as much by D'Erlon's retreat as by the disaster to Reille's divisions inflicted under the very eyes of the Marshal."
2. Simmonds' *Journal*.
3. Moorsom, *History of 52nd Light Infantry*.

To reach the bridge Vandermaesen under cover of night moved up the left bank of the river, and about 3 a.m.

.... made a desperate attack with an overwhelming force and carried it. Captain Cadoux brought his company to the bridge and tried to drive the enemy back or prevent more from passing. They fought most heroically, he soon fell, after receiving several musket balls in his breast. Several men were killed and wounded, and they were obliged to retire a little distance, but kept up a fire as long as the enemy continued to file over the river.[1]

General Skerrett commanding the brigade refused to allow Colonel Colborne to send assistance to the 95th Companies. The crossing of the bridge[2] cost the French heavy losses. General Vandermaesen, who led their attack, was killed, and 300 dead were found near the bridge in the morning besides others drowned in attempting to swim across the river.

So for the third time within ten weeks a defeated French army re-crossed the frontier, having lost 174 officers and 3,817 other ranks killed, wounded and prisoners.

On the same day at 8 a.m., 31st August, the allied batteries had opened fire on San Sebastian, and at 11 a.m. the assault commenced. By 3 p.m. the town, a considerable part of which was in flames, was taken, when General Rey, the survivors of the garrison and many British prisoners retired to the citadel on the Monte Orgullo. On the 3rd September Rey asked for a suspension of arms, but Graham refused it. On the 8th the citadel was bombarded by 59 guns, and on the 9th Rey surrendered after a siege of seventy-three days, two assaults and a loss of 1,538 men. Emmanuel Rey had been a soldier from

---

2. Simmonds, *A British Rifleman.*
3. The old bridge still stands. On it is a tablet inscribed in English and Spanish: "To the glory of God and in memory of Captain Daniel Cadoux and his gallant riflemen who on the 1st September, 1813, fell gloriously defending this bridge against the furious attack of a French division. His fame can never die." Sir Harry Smith. Erected by the Rifle Brigade and his relatives.

his fifteenth year and a general of brigade for several years, but being considered unfit for field service owing to health and infirmities, he had been relegated to the command of a district in Spain, then became Governor of Burgos, whence he was sent by King Joseph to San Sebastian on the 19th June. A very Falstaff in appearance, Sir A. Frazer describes him as "a great fat man, heavy bodied and moon faced." Nevertheless, by his spirit, resource and example, constantly on the ramparts by day and night, he had inspired his motley garrison with much of his courage and determination. When at the head of his men he marched out of the fortress with the honours of war, the veteran was saluted by every member of Graham's staff. Then he and his men sailed for England as prisoners of war. His Emperor, recognizing his gallant defence, promoted him to General of Division on the 6th November, 1813. Returning to France in 1814, he died in 1846.

CHAPTER 6

The Defence of France

The heavy losses in the Pyrenees and in the attack on San Marcial had reduced the fighting strength of the French infantry by over 17,000 men; the receipt on 2nd September of Suchet's refusal to co-operate in the proposed advance into Aragon, and the fact that the surrender of San Sebastian on the 9th had rendered the whole allied army available for a forward movement, must have made it clear to Soult that, for the present at any rate, he must remain on the defensive and therefore strengthen the positions held by his troops.

On arrival at Bayonne in July he had found the fortress in a neglected state. Besides seeing to the repair of the works and putting their armaments in order, he ordered the construction of two entrenched camps outside the fortifications; one on the heights of Mousserolles between the right bank of the Nive and the Adour, the other on the left bank of the Nive covering the main road from Bayonne into Spain; his object being "to carry the defence entirely outside (the town) and give a *point d'appui* to a field army too strong to shut itself up in the town."[1]

Later on he instructed Colonel Michaud, the chief field engineer, to draw up a project for a series of works about Bordagain, covering Ciboure,[2] and also to act as a bridgehead for the passage over the Nivelle at St. Jean de Luz.

1. Soult to Guerre, 16th July, 1813.
2. Ciboure is a suburb of St. Jean de Luz on the left bank of the Nivelle.

Michaud's proposals having been approved, work commenced towards the end of August. On the 2nd September Soult ordered the construction of a double bridge-head at Cambo. It was to be armed with 20 guns and to be strong enough to resist an *"attaque de vive force"*; as a support on the right bank of the Nive field works were to be thrown up on the slopes of the Ursouia mountain which would also cover the St. Jean Pied-de-Port road to Bayonne.[1]

For the field army Soult proposed there should be a defensive system in three lines. The first that held before and after the attack on San Marcial. The second was to have its right on the works in front of St. Jean de Luz, thence by the slopes of the Rhune mountain, the heights of Serres and those to the north of Sare and Ainhoa, the Mondarrain heights, the Cambo bridge-head and the Ursouia works. The third line was that of the River Nive, the Cambo bridge-head and its left at St. Jean Pied-de-Port. The second line was to be considered "the line of the army."[2]

All along the first line and in rear of it, soldiers and civilian workers were busy throwing up defences and improving the communications. In the area there were many works made during the Revolutionary Wars; these were repaired and others commenced.

On the 1st October Soult proceeded to St. Jean Pied-de-Port. After inspecting the existing works and the surroundings of the town, he concluded that if attacked the place could not make an effective resistance; nor could it delay an enemy's advance, as the latter's columns could everywhere pass the place beyond the range of its guns. He therefore ordered Foy to at once commence the lay-out and construction of a series of redoubts covering the exits from the Val Carlos, and these were to be finished in eight days.

---

1. By Urcuray and Mendionde. The present road in the Nive valley did not then exist. On the 4th October Soult visited the bridge-head works and considered they were then defensible. Soult to Guerre, 5th October.
2. Soult to Reille, 11th September, 1813.

These would be so advantageously placed outside the range of the guns of the citadel that I ought to be able to arrive to their assistance before the enemy can make any progress whatever force he employs.[1]

After his inspection of the defences along the line, Soult reported to the Minister that "day by day our line becomes stronger," that the moral of the troops was improved and that he was satisfied regarding their state and the works they were throwing up.[2] On the 6th October he proceeded to Espelette, where he inspected the troops, which, he said, were in a perfect state, well disposed and in good health.

The works which they are constructing along the line from the rocks of the Mondarrain to the bridge of Amots by the ridges behind and in front of Ainhoa are already defensible and will be finished in fifteen days. To-morrow (7th October) I propose to see the divisions of the centre which are in front of Sare.[3]

But on the morrow, both he and his troops were otherwise engaged.

At the beginning of October the distribution in detail from right to left of the divisions forming the corps of Generals Reille and Clausel was as follows.

Reille's corps headquarters, Chateau de Urtubie, near Urrugne. Maucune's division in first line from the sea to the Enderlazza ford over the Bidassoa and the Col du Poirier. The right section" of this front was held by Pinoteau's brigade, the 17th Light, 3rd and 15th Line, each of one battalion. The 3rd watched the estuary with a line of posts from Behobie to Hendaye, with the rest of the battalion in support on the ridge to the south of the village. The 15th held the Louis XIV hill, the 17th was in reserve on the Cafe Republicain heights.

---

1. Soult to Guerre, St. Jean Pied-de-Port, 2nd October, 1813.
2. Soult to Guerre, Bayonne, 4th October, 1813.
3. Soult to Guerre, Espelette, 6th October, 1813.

Montford's brigade carried on the line. The 10th Light,—two battalions—holding Biriatou and the Chouhille rocks with its camp on the slopes behind the church; the 101st (one battalion) at the foot of the Calvaire hill, with the two battalions of the 105th in reserve on the Croix-des-Bouquets heights. On the extreme left two battalions of the 2nd Light of the 9th Division held the Col du Poirier and the Enderlazza ford with posts along the right bank of the river below the Mandale mountain and their supports in trenches on its southern slopes. In case of attack the posts had orders to retire on their supports and both to prevent the enemy ascending.

The other division of Reille's corps, the 9th,[1] commanded on 7th October by General Boyer, was about Urrugne, and furnished working parties for the defence works at Bordagain and Ciboure. The signal arranged to give warning of an advance by the enemy was two guns fired with an interval of one minute from the Croix-des-Bouquets; when it was made the division was to assemble at once on the main road.

Clausel's corps, headquarters, Sare.

Taupin's division held the Bayonette redoubt and the entrenched camp on the summit of the mountain, the star redoubt and other works on the long spur running down towards Vera with Bechaud's brigade of five battalions. The second brigade under Colonel Cambriel held the defences thrown up about the Puerto de Vera and on the saddle ridge; the 31st Light having four companies on the Alzate Real ridge, called the *hogsback* by the British.

Conroux's division had Rey's brigade in advance watching the tracks to Vera and Echalar. The 12th Light of this brigade, two battalions, had orders to move up to the Soubicia spur of the Great Rhune immediately there was any indication of an advance by the enemy. Here it would command the Vera-Olhette road and be a support to the left of Taupin's division.

---

1. Reille's report to Soult, Soubalette, 18th October, 1813.

Clausel had impressed on his generals the necessity of blocking by abattis the paths leading to Rhune, a fairly easy matter owing to the wooded nature of the ground. "Above all things," he said, "make your dispositions before being attacked. Appoint commanders for the various posts, because in such a difficult country, every commander, knowing his general's views, ought to be himself a general and act accordingly."[1] He laid down that if obliged to retreat, Taupin was to do so towards Ascain by the western slopes of the Rhune, Conroux by the eastern to the Col D'Ignace on the road from Sare to Ascain.

Villatte's reserve division had one brigade at Ascain, two at Serres and the fourth, the Spanish brigade, at Cambo at work on the bridge-head there.

The left wing commanded by Lieutenant-General the Count D'Erlon, headquarters, Espelette.

Darmagnac's division in first line with outposts watching the country and road towards the Col de Maya, the main body of the division in the camp of Ainhoa on the ridge to the north of the village.

Abbé's division in camp between Espelette and Ainhoa. Boivin's brigade finding the garrisons of the works thrown up on the Atchulegui, Chapora and Mondarrain heights.

Darricau's division was at "this time at Ibarron on the right bank of the Nivelle, about 5 miles to north-west of Ainhoa.

Foy's division was at St. Jean Pied-de-Port.

The defence of the high valleys to the east of St. Jean was allotted to Paris's brigade of the army of Aragon and the National Guards of the Hautes Pyrenees.

---

1. Clausel to Taupin, Conroux and Maransin, 12th September, 1813.

CHAPTER 7

Wellington's Choices

As we have seen, news of the denunciation of the armistice, that Austria had joined the allies, and the intended resumption of hostilities reached Wellington about the 5th September. Writing on the 12th to Henry Wellesley, Wellington told him that there was a French report of a victory gained by Napoleon at Dresden on the 26th August, that he considered, from what he had seen in a copy of the *Moniteur*[1] of 6th September, that the affair was one of no great consequence, and was probably only a reconnaissance. But this gave him the assurance he required, "that hostilities had really been renewed in Germany,"[2] which was corroborated by the news received on the 16th September of the disaster on the 31st August to Vandamme's corps, and on the 25th of the French defeats on the Elbe and in Silesia.[3]

San Sebastian having surrendered on 9th September, the whole allied army, except the two Spanish divisions blockading Pamplona, was available for such action as Wellington had stated

---

1. The French Government publication. He seems to have received this regularly from an individual whom he terms "My correspondent in Bayonne." Wellington to Bathurst, 8th October, 1813.
2. Wellington to Bathurst, 23rd August, 1813. "I shall do all in my power to draw the attention of the enemy to this quarter as soon as I know that hostilities are really renewed in Germany."
3. Wellington to H. Wellesley, 16th September, and to Beresford, 25th September. "No new light has been thrown on the battles on the Elbe, but I think Bonaparte was beaten in Silesia and by Bernadotte on his left."

he would take "to draw the enemy's attention to this quarter." Moreover, an early advance would come at a propitious time as "Vandamme's defeat recovered the credit of the Allies, and has put them again into decent good humour with each other."[1]

It may be useful here to consider what possible courses of action were open to Wellington, and to give his views, so far as is possible, regarding the various alternatives. Speaking generally, there appear to have been two, namely a general advance into France, seeking a decisive battle with Soult and having Bayonne and the line of the River Adour as objective, or a less ambitious programme with a nearer objective, from which, when gained and consolidated, either a further advance could be made or the matter put to the test of a general engagement.

If the first course was adopted, concentration of the allied army in some form would be necessary owing to its extended front of some 35 miles. This would have to be arranged according to the intended line or lines of advance of the main portion of the army. If towards the right, with the object of turning the left of the French entrenched line obliging Soult to retire with the possibility also of cutting him off from Bayonne; the left of the allied line would necessarily have to be weakened, thereby impairing the security of the allied harbours and bases on which the army depended for all its supplies, and would open a long line of communication and supply over difficult country and requiring strong protection. Such a move was not likely to be favoured by Wellington under the circumstances then existing. He would not risk his communication with the sea.[2] Concentration in force towards the left would leave open the communication

---

1. Bathurst to Wellington, 8th October, 1813.
2. Wellington to Lord W. Bentinck, 14th August, 1813. "The great difficulty I have always found in the Peninsula has been the subsistence of the army. In order to supply this and other numerous wants, I have never ventured to risk even the communication with the sea." An undated memo, signed by Wellington "about a forward movement of the right of the army during winter of 1813/14," shows he had considered such a move, but this was later on and under different circumstances.

between St. Jean Pied-de-Port and Pamplona and thereby imperil the blockade of that fortress unless a strong force was left to hold the passes about Roncevaux. It would also open direct communication, and possibly combined action, between Soult and Suchet. This appears to have been Wellington's view. Writing to Graham on 5th October he said, "From what we can make out of an intercepted letter from the Governor of Pamplona I judge he can hold out till 20th or 25th, and till that time we certainly cannot move our right." If concentration was towards the centre, it would be the easiest carried out, and probably the least dangerous; but again the protection of the flanks would have to be assured with a corresponding diminution in strength of the attacking force. As will be seen later, this was the concentration Wellington adopted prior to the battle of the Nivelle, Pamplona having surrendered in the meantime.

Moreover, in the hilly and undulating country lying between the allied position and the Adour, the chances of gaining a decisive victory with the armament of those days were not great; for behind every position taken up there will be found another, generally just as good, to which the enemy could retreat,[1] and the country is such that cavalry could not be employed in large bodies, and difficult for the artillery of those days.

Having considered the situation, Wellington decided that, until Pamplona surrendered, no general advance of his army could be made. He, as has been stated in his own words, realized that, in the existing circumstances, his duty to his army, his Government and the allied Powers, obliged him "to proceed with caution." He was not going to risk all his chances in one battle in which, owing to the nature of the country, he could not count on a decisive victory; and it was important that no mishap to his army should occur to discourage the allies in

---

1. Wellington to Bathurst, 18th October, 1813. "Unless I could fight a general action with Soult and gain a complete victory, which the nature of the country would scarcely admit of."

the north. He considered he could best aid the general cause by a carefully considered step-by-step advance, each move to be within his means, and backed up by all he could put into the problem, surprise—the enemy's greatest foe—right direction and right concentration of strength. He was confident that what he ordered his troops could and would do; whilst they on their part had equal confidence that what they were ordered to do was the best way of doing the job.

His scheme in outline was to throw his left wing across the lower Bidassoa and its estuary, and seize the line of hills which dominate the right bank of that river, whilst his left centre captured the Grande Rhune mountain and the high ground to the west of it. By so doing, he would get the left wing out of the unfavourable position it was obliged to maintain so long as the siege of San Sebastian went on, overlooked as it was on every side from the French position on the hills across the river,[1] which also commanded the valley road on the left bank,[2] and obliged all communication between the centre and left of the army to be carried on by steep and narrow tracks from Lesaca over the Haya mountain to Irun and Oyarzun. Possession of this road would greatly facilitate communication and supply; and that of the heights would give better protection to the harbours and a stronger position against any attempt Soult might make to advance by the great road. Whilst another harbour, that of Fuenterabia, would be gained, an indifferent one and useless in the winter, but which, as long as the weather held up, might prove useful as an adjunct to the hard-worked land transport.

The capture of the Grande Rhune mountain would: se-

---

1. Wellington to Graham, 5th October, 1813. "The heights on the right bank of the Bidassoa command such a view over us that we must have them, and the sooner the better."
2. Graham to Wellington, 5th July, 1813. "The French have small camps on all the projecting points, which in many cases command the road on this Hide of the river where the valley is very narrow. It is, however, a good car road wide enough for artillery."

cure an advanced offensive position right in the centre of the French entrenched line and one commanding the routes leading thereto. Moreover, its summit, rising to nearly 3,000 feet, stands like a watch tower from which can be viewed all the country between the Pyrenees and Bayonne.

Wellington had intended to make his move as soon as possible after the surrender of San Sebastian,[1] but an unfortunate incident delayed the advance. With the assistance of Spanish fishermen several fords across the lower course of the Bidassoa and its estuary had been; located, but most of them in the estuary were passable for infantry only at dead low water of spring tides, which here rise 16 feet. The only bridge between Vera and the sea, that by which the great road crossed the Bidassoa at Behobie, had been destroyed by the French. For the passage of artillery, and indeed for the safety and supply of the force, after its crossing, temporary bridges were necessary, and for these the presence of the pontoon train, then some 60 miles to the rear at Vitoria, was essential.

The moon would be new on 23rd September, and near about this date would be the highest and lowest tides[2] and therefore suitable for the crossing. On the 10th September the chief engineer was directed to send order to the officer in charge of the train to move up at once to Oyarzun. On making inquiry as to its movements Wellington learnt on the 17th that:

> .... the chief engineer is not now certain as to whether the orders he sent have reached the officer in charge, and has taken no measures to repeat them. He put his letter into the Spanish post office—I conclude addressed in English—and without knowing if the officer in charge is in communication with that post office, and there he left it. This is the way our arrangements fail. Officers charged to send an order will not attend to that essential part of their duty, the mode of transmitting it.[2]

---

1. Wellington to Bathurst, 19th September, 1813. 2. Nautical Almanac, 1813.
2. Wellington to Graham, Lesaca, 17th September, 1813.

The chief engineer was ordered to send an officer riding post-haste with fresh orders; but the movement of the army had to be postponed till about the full moon, which would be on 9th October.[1]

During September Wellington had ordered the 3rd Spanish Army, three divisions, about 12,000 men, under the Duque del Parque, to move up to Tudela, where it arrived on the 15th. One division was sent on to Pamplona to relieve the Andalusian division of Giron's corps, which then rejoined its corps at Echalar. Ostensibly the move of the 3rd Army was to strengthen the allied right; doubtless it was also intended to come to the knowledge of Soult. Early in October Mina moved up the Irati valley close to Hill's right, and on 1st October Wellington himself went to Roncevaux and on the way caused Campbell's brigade of the Portuguese Division in the Alduides to raid some French posts in the Baigorry valley. These movements, Wellington's presence at Roncevaux and the false intelligence, probably put about by his agents, tended to confirm Soult that the allied attack would be made against his left and left centre, notwithstanding his knowledge that the allied pontoon train was moving up to the front, and the information he had from deserters and spies that the attack would be against his right and the Rhune mountain. Writing to the War Minister on the 18th October, after the action, he said, "I had several reasons to believe that the enemy's principal attack would be on Ainhoa," but is careful not to state them. He probably reckoned that when Wellington did advance it would be with all his forces and by his right so as to turn the French defended line and oblige him to retreat.

As it was found that the tide would serve on the 7th October,[2] that date was fixed for the movement, and the orders issued on the 5th. These are given in an abbreviated form in the following chapter.

---

1. Nautical Almanac, 1813.
2. Full moon was on the 9th October, 1813.

CHAPTER 8

Plans to Advance

The Portuguese Division in the Alduides valley to move at daybreak on the 7th instant to Errazu and occupy the positions now held by the 3rd Division in the Maya valley. Lieut.-General Sir R. Hill to make such arrangements as he considers necessary to replace the Portuguese Division, and if he considers it necessary, he is authorized to call on General Mina to strengthen his right flank.

One brigade of the 3rd Division is to move at daybreak on 7th, and occupy the heights overlooking the village of Zugaramurdi; to be followed by the other brigade as soon as the Portuguese Division approaches. The G.O.C. 7th Division to send an officer acquainted with the country to the 3rd Division as a guide.

The G.O.C. 7th Division will move his two rear brigades at daybreak on 7th to the Spanish encampment in the Puerto de Echalar, their tents to remain standing till 7 a.m. The brigade in advance about Zugaramurdi to maintain its position until the approach of the 3rd Division, when it will move and rejoin the remainder of the division in the Puerto de Echalar.

The left of the enemy's position is to be attacked by General Giron's Spanish corps, which will advance in two columns whose objectives will be the two extremities of a wooded bank which extends from the Grande Rhune mountain towards the rocks on the left flank of the enemy's encampment in the Puerto de Vera, the line of advance of the right column being by roads which appear of a red earthy colour and ascend on our right of the wooded bank already mentioned. The left column is to move so as to pass through a ravine which is at the extremity of steep ridge on which the enemy has an outpost and which is particularly marked by a zigzag path a little to our left of the ravine mentioned. After entering the ravine the column will ascend the wooded bank by roads of a whitish colour which lead up to that end of the bank next the rocks on the left of the enemy's encampment in the Puerto de Vera.

To aid the operations of these two columns General Giron will detach as early as possible one battalion from the right column with orders to move up through the woods on the lower slopes of the Grande Rhune, concealing its movements as much as possible. This battalion will endeavour to gain the summit of the Rhune, and also a spur therefrom, which appears to command the left flank and to some extent the rear of the enemy's position in the Puerto de Vera.

General Giron will have two battalions in reserve during the attack; and one brigade is to be posted towards the entrance of the valley of Vera from Sare to cover the right flank and rear of the attacking troops. The skirmishers, of the left column are to keep communication with those on the right of the Light Division.

All arrangements for these operations are to commence at daybreak on 7th instant, and the troops will advance at 7 a.m. exactly. The Spanish posts in the Puerto de Echalar will, however, remain there till relieved by the 7th Division.

Attack on Centre and Right of Enemy's Position Above Vera— to be Made by Light Division and General Longa's Division

One part of Light Division will operate directly against the enemy's encampment in the Puerto de Vera. This attack to extend on its right as far as the rocks on the left flank of this encampment, and will get into communication with the left column of Giron's corps. The remainder of the Light Division will gain the heights above the Church of Vera, and then advance against the enemy's right encampment.

Major-General Alten will leave such reserves as he considers necessary on the narrow rocky ridge to our right of the Puerto de Vera and on the heights above the Church of Vera. The Light Division to advance half an hour after that of the Spanish corps.

Half of General Longa's troops will pass the Bidassoa by the bridge of Vera and will move forward into the great wooded ravine which lies between the enemy's right and centre encampments. These troops will connect the two attacking columns of the Light Division, and will aid their advance by pushing forward a great number of skirmishers through the woods to act against the flanks and rear of the enemy on both sides of the ravine. The other half of Longa's troops will pass the Bidassoa by the fords near Zalain, and will act against the right encampments of the enemy in co-operation with the left column of the Light Division. These troops will push forward as many skirmishers as possible, endeavouring always to turn the right of the enemy in whatever positions he takes up. General Longa will also detach a few companies to pass the Bidassoa near Enderlazza, and then ascend the hill on which the French telegraph is situated. He will communicate with General Alten, and form all his arrangements for these operations in concert with that officer, who will have the general superintendence of both divisions during the attack.

The 4th Division will move from Lesaca soon after daybreak, and will be in reserve on Santa Barbara heights during the attack.

The 6th Division will remain in its positions in the Puerto de Maya during the operations; but Major-General Colville will make such demonstrations as will keep the enemy in uncertainty, and prevent his detaching any considerable part of his force from the positions he holds about Ainhoa.

Movements of the Left of the Army

The 5th Division with one squadron of 12th Light Dragoons and the battery of artillery attached to the division will pass the Bidassoa by the fords near Fuenterabia. A battery from the reserve artillery will also move to Fuenterabia, and will act as may be necessary during the passage of the troops, and will afterwards remain in reserve on the left bank of the river. The above-mentioned troops must move to Fuenterabia so as to arrive there and be placed before daybreak on the 7th instant in the ditch of the place and in other situations where they cannot be seen by the enemy. They are to advance and commence passing the fords as soon as the tide has fallen sufficiently to admit of their doing so, which will probably be about 7.15 a.m. As they arrive on the opposite bank, they will occupy the high ground in their front, and will afterwards move to their right so as to threaten the right flank of the enemy's force opposed to the troops which are to pass the river near the ruined bridge, and the 5th Division is to connect with these troops as soon as possible. Major Todd, Royal Staff Corps, is to accompany this column.

The 1st Division and Wilson's Portuguese brigade will cross the Bidassoa by the ford at the ruined bridge, No. 6, and by two fords a little lower down the river, Nos. 4 and 5; a part of this force will also cross at ford No. 7, a short distance above the bridge. These troops will begin to advance towards

70

the fords at the same time that the troops at Fuenterabia move forward. A signal previously agreed upon must therefore be made from Fuenterabia.[1] The remainder of the 12th Light Dragoons, the 1st Division battery and the Royal Staff Corps[2] will accompany this column. Its first objective is the Louis XIV hill and other advantageous points on the right bank, and it will gain connection with the 5th Division as soon as possible. The troops composing this column are to be assembled before daybreak near Irun, and in such other places as are considered advantageous, and are to be kept concealed from the enemy until they move towards the fords.

A pontoon bridge is to be thrown across the river near the ruined bridge as soon as it is possible to establish it. To cover its construction and the passage of the troops, the 18-pounder battery and two other batteries are to be placed on the San Marcial heights and in such other places as the officer commanding the artillery may direct. This artillery is to be moved during the night 6th/7th October to the vicinity of the selected places. The pontoon train is to move forward on 6th so as to reach Irun after dusk and be placed in a concealed position, where it will remain till ordered forward towards the river.

The tents of the 1st and 5th Divisions and other troops of the left wing are to be left standing, and all baggage is to remain in the camps until all the troops are firmly established on the right bank of the Bidassoa.

The Spanish troops of Lieut.-General Freyre's corps will cross the Bidassoa in the following manner. The left column will cross at ford No. 8, and will immediately occupy the

---

1. This order appears to have been modified later. Batty says: "Owing to the considerable bend of the river below bridge at Behobie, it was necessary that the 5th Division should be the first to cross, and as soon as it should be sufficiently advanced, the other columns of the 1st Division were directed to cross, and the whole corps to advance up the heights together." The signal agreed upon was a rocket to be fired from the Church tower of Fuenterabia.

2. The Royal Staff Corps were the military mounted police of the army.

71

height above the ford on which is a large tiled building with a camp of huts near it; this column will communicate on its left with the troops which cross at ford No. 7. The next column will cross at fords Nos. 9 and 10, its left to communicate with the column crossing at ford No. 8, and will assist it in occupying the heights on which are the tiled building and hutted camp already mentioned. The centre will push forward and occupy the hill called La Montagne Verte, and the right will occupy the ravine between the Montagne Verte and the Montagne Mandale, a reserve for the centre to be left at the village of Biriatou. The remainder of General Freyre's troops will pass the river at fords Nos. 11, 12 and 13. Their objective will be the summit of the Mandale mountain, where they will establish themselves firmly, and form an *appui* on the right flank to the whole of the operations of the left wing of the army. The troops on the extreme right of the Spanish Corps will move up the ravine which is to the right of the Mandale, and which separates it from the narrow rocky hill (Licarlan) on its right.

The crossing of the Spanish troops will be supported by the Spanish artillery and by two batteries of British artillery; the guns to be moved on the night of 6th/7th near the positions where they are to come into action.

A pontoon bridge will be established as early as possible at a point, which has been selected, a short distance below ford No. 9. The pontoons to be moved during the night 6th/7th to a position to be selected by the officer in charge of the train.

Lieut.-General Sir T. Graham will arrange with Lieut.-General Freyre for a signal to be made from Irun when the 1st Division advances; the Spanish troops will be put in motion at the same time.

Bradford's Portuguese brigade will move at daybreak on the 7th, and be placed on the right of the San Marcial position as a reserve.

Aylmer's brigade will move so as to be before daylight in the valley behind the San Marcial position. It will form the reserve to the 1st Division, and will be placed to the left of the San Marcial position near the high road between Irun and the ruined bridge, when the 1st Division advances.

Lieut.-General Sir T. Graham will give orders for such detachments being furnished as may be required to assist the pontoon train and the artillery in moving to their positions. He will also communicate the necessary orders concerning the above arrangements for the left of the army to all the troops concerned, except the Spanish troops, for whom a separate copy of the instructions (in French) has been sent to Lieut.-General Freyre.

(Signed) *G. Murray, Q.M.G.*

CHAPTER 9

The Crossing of the Bidassoa

Before entering into the details of the crossing and subsequent events, it may be well to describe briefly the general nature of the country about to be fought over. From accounts and letters of the period British officers appear to have been impressed with the contrast this country presented to the average Spanish country they had hitherto been journeying over. In a letter to his wife Sir A. Frazer thus describes it:

> The part of France we have entered is hilly, or rather less mountainous than the Pyrenees, but except towards the Nivelle is anything but flat. There are hedgerows like those in England; in short, already we see a different country ..
> .. The country changes the moment one has crossed the Bidassoa at Irun, hedges appear and the heathy country interspersed with fields reminds one of England.[1]

That part of the area which lies to the north of the Irun-Bayonne road maintains the heather type of country which Frazer mentions, except in the immediate vicinity of Hendaye where there is a good deal of wood, and which, is now much built over. Rounded ridges and valleys abound, the latter generally narrow with steep sides: I in the lower parts there is considerable cultivation, maize, wheat, vines and grassland, the fields mostly enclosed by growing hedges, but the higher ground is rough grass, heather,

1. Lieut.-Colonel Sir Augustus Frazer, then commanding the Royal Horse Artillery, Vera; 10th October, 1813.

74

bracken and gorse with patches of wood in places, and, with the exception of new roads, buildings, rail and tramways, is probably very much the same as it was in 1813.

On the south of the main road the line of hills on the right bank of the Bidassoa, extending from the Bayonnette mountain (1,900 ft.), by the Mandale (1,613 ft.), the Chouhille rocks (1,175 ft.), Lumaferde (520 ft.), the Green hill (370 ft.) to the Louis XIV (410 ft.) above Behobie, stands like a wall as if blocking entrance into France. But there are gaps in it by which entrance can be gained. The Louis XIV hill, the rocky front of which rises almost perpendicularly from the river, can be turned by its flanks, and the depression between it and the northern end of the Green hill gives an opening for an advance against the slopes and the southern end of the Croix-des-Bouquets heights and also towards Urrugne. Possession of the Biriatou plateau and the Chouhille heights turns the southern end of the Green hill and the Lumaferde, opening a line of advance towards the Calvaire mountain and into the comparatively level ground lying south of the main road as far as the lower northern slopes of the great Rhune. Capture of the Col du Poirier turns all the defences of the Mandale and those of the western end of the Bayonnette; and opens a way by mountain paths towards Olhette and the Urrugne-Jolimont-Ascain road.

The 6th of October had been an intensely hot day. In the evening heavy masses of cloud gathered over the mountains casting a deep gloom over the whole country, and at length burst into a violent thunderstorm accompanied by rain and hail. Towards morning the storm passed over to the French side of the river.[1]

By 3 a.m. on the 7th the troops were under arms and began to move to their assigned positions. 5th Division from left to right. Robinson's brigade, one squadron 12th Light Dragoons, Mosse's and Cairne's batteries of artillery and 300 men

---

1. Batty, *Campaign of Western Pyrenees.*

of the 3rd Portuguese detached from the Portuguese brigade were concealed behind Fuenterabia and the fishermen's cottages to the north of it. Major-General Hay, commanding the division, was with this column.[1]

The Portuguese brigade under Colonel de Regoa and on its right the 1st Brigade, commanded by Colonel Hon. C. Greville, were concealed behind embankments, raised to protect the meadows and cultivated ground from the tide, opposite fords 2 and 3, these being in front of a large white building, a Capuchin convent.

The 1st Division; the 2nd Guards brigade, Major-General Stopford, and the King's German Legion troops behind an underfeature springing from the northern slope of the San Marcial heights, on which stand the ruins of the Chateau de Behobie, and running for about a mile parallel to the Irun-Behobie road and the river. The 1st Guards brigade, Colonel Maitland, and Wilson's Portuguese brigade were behind San Marcial heights, with Aylmer's brigade in rear of them. The 3rd, 4th and 5th Divisions of the 4th Spanish Army on the San Marcial heights, with Bradford's Portuguese brigade in rear of their right.

Besides the artillery with the divisions, three guns of the 18-pounder battery with an infantry escort were in an entrenchment, which had been previously thrown up, on the underfeature previously mentioned, which commanded the loop-holed houses occupied by the French piquet guarding the ford close to the broken bridge. Ross's troop of horse artillery was behind the San Marcial spur ready to cover the crossing of the 2nd Guards and German Legion troops. On the San Marcial heights were Ramsay's troop, J. Michell's battery and a troop of Spanish horse artillery.

At about 7.30 a.m. the tide was sufficiently low to render the fords passable, and the columns of the 5th Division issued from their concealment and commenced to cross the estuary. The left column from Fuenterabia made for the long spit of sand jutting

---

1. Hay's Report, 8th October, 1813.

out from the heights about Ste. Anne, on which now stand the casino, hotels and villas of Hendaye Plage. This column appears to have met with no resistance until fired on from a battery of 24-pounders on the heights above the beach.

The Portuguese brigade and that of Colonel Greville on the right moved straight across by fords 2 and 3 towards the slopes on the right bank south of Hendaye. Captain Malcolm,[1] who was with the light companies [2] of Greville's brigade, thus describes their move into position and subsequent advance.[1]

About midnight we descended from the hills and ravines skirted with woods and marched in profound silence towards the Bidassoa over the meadow ground below Fuenterabia. On the Spanish side of the river was erected a broad and pretty high wall of turf with a ditch behind it; we moved on in silence till we reached the wall and concealed ourselves in the ditch, while our pioneers with the greatest possible silence cut several large openings in the wall through which we might pass. The storm had died away, the moon had set and though there were stars visible the night was unusually dark. One sound only was heard, and it made the surrounding silence more visibly felt. It was the noise of the cannon and pontoons rolling up from the rear deep and heavy as the moan of a torrent or the sound of a distant sea . . . .[3] We (the light companies) rushed out at the openings made by the pioneers and dashed into the water.[4] It was middle deep, so that the men had to

1. Captain J. Malcolm, *Campaigns in Pyrenees and South of France.*
2. In the Peninsular Army the light companies of each brigade with the attached rifle company when in action formed a battalion under a Field Officer of the brigade.
3. Though the guns and pontoon train had been ordered to be at Irun after dusk, "the road was so blocked up that, though the distance from Oyarzun to Irun is only two leagues, it was daylight before we reached the latter." Frazer's letter, 8th October.
4. The Light Company of the 3rd Royal Scots, commanded by Lieut. J. N. Ingram, was the first to enter France.

hold up their arms and ammunition. Our plunge into the water was echoed by the fire of the French sentries, who having fired retreated with the utmost rapidity. Their outpost took the alarm, and collecting among the orchards and undulating ground commenced a hot skirmish with the light companies."

The French troops here were two companies of the 3rd Line in support of the piquets. Unable to hold the ground, they fell back on the main body of the battalion posted on the slopes south of Hendaye. Pushing on the British and Portuguese light troops attacked the 3rd and drove it back towards the cafe republicain ridge.

Meanwhile at 8 a.m.,[1] the signal rocket having been fired from Fuenterabia and white flag displayed on the San Marcial chapel, the 1st Division and the Spaniards began to move and the 18-pounder guns and those on San Marcial opened fire. The German legion troops, preceded by their light infantry brigade, commenced to cross by the ford near the broken bridge. Entering the water at the wrong spot the light infantry got into deep water, but regaining the line got safely over, then extending with their right on the main road they covered the crossing of the line regiments and the 2nd Guards brigade which crossed lower down by the Jonco ford.

The 1st Guards brigade and Wilson's Portuguese moved over the San Marcial heights and crossed the river near the gap at the south end of the Louis XIV hill.

The 4th Spanish Army columns assembled towards the southern end of the San Marcial heights, as soon as the signal to move was displayed "as if impatient rushed down the mountain a little to the right, east of Biriatou, and forded the river."[2]

The left and left centre columns had a sharp fight with

---

1. Frazer's letter of 8th October. "The affair began at 8 a.m."
2. Frazer's letter of 8th October. Lieut.-Colonel Frazer was with the artillery on the heights. Batty says the howitzer fire of the British batteries (each had one 5½-inch howitzer) did "essential service in clearing away the enemy's piquets from the bank of the river."

the enemy's troops holding the village and the ridge on which was "the tiled roof building" and their hutted camp; but meanwhile the other columns having forded the river were ascending the steep slopes of the Chouhille and Mandale heights and were driving the French piquets from their trenches on the slopes, whilst the column on the extreme right was making its way up the Licarlan ravine towards the Col du Poirier.

It is now time to turn to the happenings on the French side as given in Reille's report on the action.[1] General Montfort's report that he had observed movements in the allied camps having reached Reille at about 7.30 a.m., he immediately ordered the 9th, Boyer's, Division to get under arms and assemble in front of its camps. About a quarter of an hour later, having heard the signal guns fired from the Croix-des-Bouquets, he ordered the 9th Division to move there, and himself rode off at once to the Louis XIV hill, distant about 4 miles. On arrival, probably soon after 8 a.m., he found the 1st Division crossing near the broken bridge and at the Jonco ford under the protection of their skirmishers and the allied artillery; that another division which, he said, he had since learnt was the 5th Division[2] was passing opposite Hendaye and by the coast line, which appeared to be supported by the 4th Division[2] crossing the river near a large white building (the Capuchin convent), whilst the 4th Spanish Army divisions were crossing by the fords below and above Biriatou. The French artillery on the cafe republicain and on the main road were in action against the enemy, but the latter, taking advantage of the broken ground, had driven back the two advanced companies of the 3rd Line, and then aided by another column on its left (de Regoa's Portuguese brigade), had driven back the 3rd Line from its position in rear, whilst the 5th Division being

1. Reille to Soult, Soubalette, 18th October, 1813.
2. Reille was of course mistaken here. What he took to be the 4th Division was Greville's and de Regoa's brigades, and what he calls the 5th, was Robinson's brigade of that division with guns and cavalry.

unopposed about Hendaye was advancing along the coast. To meet this threat against the right of the Croix-des-Bouquets position, Reille sent an order to Boyer to detach a battalion to occupy some old entrenchments of the Revolutionary war on the long spur running north-eastwards from the northern end of the Croix-des-Bouquets ridge, which were known as the camp des Sans Culottes.

Reille's stay on the Louis XIV hill can only have been a short one, for by now the advance of the German legion had obliged the French guns to retire from the main road, Wilson's Portuguese and the 1st Guards brigade were crossing below the hill and the Spaniards attacking Biriatou, so he was no doubt obliged to leave the hill and return to the Croix-des-Bouquets.

Meanwhile Greville's and de Regoa's brigades, covered by their light companies and cacadores, continued their advance, the French 3rd falling back on the 17th which held an entrenched camp on the cafe republicain. Here the French made a spirited resistance, holding up the light companies, and the camp was not taken until the Royal Scots and 38th regiments were brought up to their assistance. Greville now got into touch with the 1st Division, which was advancing on both sides of the main road, the French 3rd, 15th and 17th regiments falling back towards the Croix-des-Bouquets ridge held by two battalions of the 105th.

Robinson's column on the extreme left continued to move along the coast. Having captured the battery on the Ste. Anne heights, which was rushed by a detachment of the 47th Regiment and a company of the 3rd Portuguese, the column changed direction half right, crossed the stream in the valley below and moved towards the Sans Culottes entrenchments.

On the San Marcial side, the 1st Guards brigade and Wilson's Portuguese had seized the Louis XIV hill; the left and left centre Spanish columns were stoutly opposed by the 10th Light about Biriatou; but its left flank being turned by the Spanish centre column, which had gained the Chouhille rocks above the village, the 10th retired, leaving on the ground four guns which had been in action on their left. The other Spanish columns, having driven the French piquets from their trenches on the slopes of the Mandale, had gained its summit.

It was now about 9 a.m. In his letter of 8th October, Frazer writes:

> During this time (the advance of the Spanish columns), our guns and those of the Spanish horse artillery played on the enemy; but he made only a feeble resistance; at 9 o'clock the burning of the huts of the mountain posts showed he had abandoned them. Finding that the affair was losing all appearance of becoming serious on our right, I quitted Ramsay's and Michell's batteries, sending them orders to cross at the burnt bridge of Irun and crossed it myself at this point. The moment after I had crossed I saw the Marquis approaching the ford.... At this time the enemy had retired from the river at all points and had fallen back on what I presumed to be his second line, from a redoubt on which he opened a fire of a few guns.

With Reille on the Croix-des-Bouquets were the two battalions of the 105th, and towards it the three beaten battalions of Pinoteau's brigade were hastening. Seeing that Robinson's column was crossing the Ste. Anne heights, Reille, fearing lest the 24th, which he had ordered Boyer to detach to hold the Sans Culottes works, should not reach them before the enemy did, sent one of the 105th battalions to occupy them. For the time being, therefore, the ridge was held by one battalion only. The 1st brigade of 9th Division, with the 118th, 3 battalions, leading, was approaching from Urrugne, but was yet at a considerable distance, and the 2nd brigade had not passed Urrugne.

Now began the general advance against the French position on the Croix-des-Bouquets ridge. Even on the actual ground it is not easy to reconstruct the details of the fighting as given by Napier, but taking Greville's report, other British accounts and Reille's report, it would seem as if they were generally as follows:—The ridge was held by one battalion of 105th, the rallied 3rd, 15th and 17th French regiments with a few guns. Against the position the 1st Division, with the German legion troops leading, was advancing on both sides of the main road. Greville's brigade was advancing in an echelon of half-battalion columns with its left, the 9th Regiment, in front, his intention being, as stated in his report,[1] to gain the extreme northern end of the ridge where it falls towards the valley of the stream which enters the sea to the east of Ste. Anne's Point. On his left was the Portuguese brigade, and on his right the German Legion, which had suffered severely and had been brought to a standstill. The 9th Regiment, the two columns of which formed Greville's left, on gaining the northern slope of the Croix-des-Bouquets ridge, changed front to the right and advanced along it against the enemy's redoubt which covered the right of the French encampment on the hill.[2] The 9th were strongly opposed and had many casualties, but the redoubt was taken and the French were driven back to the main road.

Meanwhile Wilson's Portuguese and the Spanish left column pursued the 10th Light which had fallen back towards the camp held by the 101st below the Calvaire hill. Here they were attacked by Wilson and the Spaniards, and the 10th and 101st, after setting fire to their camp, retired across country towards the entrenchments south of Urrugne known as the camp des Gendarmes. The extreme right Spanish column

---

1. Greville to Hay. "I deemed it best to gain the heights yet occupied by the enemy by ascending the extreme right (enemy's) of the hill gaining a connection with Colonel de Regoa. With this intention I directed an advance in echelon from my left wings of battalions which was led in a conspicuous manner by Lieut.-Colonel Cameron, 9th Regiment, who drove in the advanced parties of the enemy."
2. This large redoubt stood about 400 yards to the north of the point where the main road from Behobie reaches the ridge; the entrenched camp was to the south of this point.

had driven the French 2nd from the Col du Poirier, which also retired towards the camp des Gendarmes, and, together with the column on the Mandale, had commenced to move across the hills towards Joliment, near which hamlet the track from the Bayonnette joins the Ascain-Urrugne road, and Olhette. On the other flank Robinson's brigade was nearing the Sans Culottes.

According to Reille's report the situation on the Croix-des-Bouquets was as follows[1]:

The British attacked the Croix-des-Bouquets in front and by the easy slopes rising from the coast, in spite of the fire of our artillery, and had seized the heights to the right of the road and were there forming opposite to the 105th, which was in line on the heights to the left, having on its flanks such portions of the three battalions of the brigade as had rallied. It was at this moment that the 118th[2] reached the top of the spur which leads to the Croix-des-Bouquets, the 24th had moved towards the right, and the 2nd brigade of the 9th Division was still at Urrugne. The head of the 118th was then about ten minutes' march from the Croix-des-Bouquets. On one flank I could see that a fight had been going on for a quarter of an hour about the camp of the 101st (Calvaire) which showed that the enemy were in possession of Biriatou and the Chouhille rocks and that my left was turned; on my right the left British column (Robinson) continued to advance. Having no hope of being able to retake the northern part of the Croix-des-Bouquets, and still less of being able to remain on the position, I ordered General Boyer to retire and form the 118th on the heights of the Chapel of Socorry, and cover the retreat of Maucune's division.

1. Reille to Soult, 18th October, 1813.
2. The 118th had three battalions, but was only about two-thirds of its strength because the men who had gone to work on the defences at 6 a.m. and the usual fatigue parties had not joined before the regiment marched.

After capturing the redoubt on the right of the French position Colonel Cameron reformed the 9th and advanced in a single column along the ridge towards the 105th battalion which had reformed about the dip in the ridge over which the main road passes. From here, owing to the shape of the ground, the 105th was able to pour a converging fire on the advancing 9th, whilst the three regiments of Pinoteau's brigade and the guns fled down the northern slopes of the ridge towards Urrugne. Though suffering heavy loss that gallant regiment was not to be denied; raising "a furious shout" it charged down on the 105th,[1] which did not meet it, but broke and followed the other regiments, and the Croix-des-Bouquets ridge was won.

Wellington[2] now appeared on the captured ridge. Frazer writes:

> On ascending the hill we found our troops formed somewhat in advance of it. An instantaneous hurrah burst from the line on seeing Lord Wellington, who rode a little to the left, where the enemy showed a feeble line disputing (with Robinson's brigade) some wooded ground. He thanked the 9th Regiment on the field for their gallant conduct.

Covered by the light companies the allied columns followed in pursuit of the French, and:

> . . . . the skirmishing became as hot as ever, the enemy at this time opened a heavy cannonade on our columns, but at that moment our horse artillery came up at a gallop and opened such a destructive fire on the enemy

---

1. In his report Reille gave this battalion high praise. "The 105th battalion stayed the enemy's efforts for a few minutes, giving the artillery and other troops time to retire down the heights. I cannot sufficiently praise the conduct of this battalion and of its commander, Colonel Mautmont."
2. Gleig, *The Subaltern*. "His dress was a plain grey frock buttoned to the, chin, a cocked hat covered with oilskin, grey pantaloons with boots buckled at the sides and a steel-mounted sabre."

that they soon gave way in all directions. We did not pursue them far, being called back by the sound of the bugle."[1]

Some of the German legion troops entered Urrugne, but were driven out of it by the second brigade of Boyer's division and French gunfire which set fire to part of the village at about 11.30 a.m.

Having gained the strong positions covering the river crossings, Wellington decided to proceed no further, and "at half-past twelve the affair ended by our assuming a position a little retired and nearly on the same one on which the second line of the enemy had rested in the morning." [2]

By the evening the allied left wing had taken up a line as follows. The three divisions of the 4th Spanish Army held the Mandale heights, on their left was Wilson's Portuguese brigade in the French camp below the Calvaire hill, which they had taken in the morning: then came Maitland's Guards brigade of the 1st Division on the Croix-des-Bouquets ridge south of the main road with the German legion line brigade to the north of it. On the left of this brigade was Stopford's Guards brigade: the remainder of the ground from thence to the sea was held by the 5th Division and the German light brigade. In the rear of this line as a reserve Aylmer's brigade and Bradford's Portuguese were on the high ground above Hendaye.

> As soon as the action was over, a line was, as if by mutual consent, agreed upon for the positions of the outposts of the two armies; the French keeping possession of Urrugne and of a hill on its right on which stands a small chapel (Socorry).[1]

The outposts of the allied left wing were in contact with the French along the line, Socorry, Urrugne and in the Olhette valley, where the village was held by the Spaniards.

1. Malcolm, *Campaign in Pyrenees and South of France.*
2. Frazer, Letter of 8th October, 1813.
3. Batty.

CHAPTER 10

The Attack on Vera

From early dawn on the 7th October the vale of Vera was being filled with troops. Giron's Spanish corps from their camps on the Ibantelly heights, the Light Division from the Santa Barbara hill, Longa's Spanish division from across the Bidassoa and the 4th Division collecting on Santa Barbara to replace the Light. As viewed from the Bayonnette the allied concentration gave its observers "no indication of an offensive movement";[1] to them it seemed as if the Light Division was about to have a drill exercise or an inspection.

Taupin, whose division had been under arms since sunrise, was about to dismiss it, but, thinking better of it, kept his men at their posts and sent a report to Clausel of what he had seen. About 7.30 a.m. the sound of musketry in the direction of Urdax and of gunfire about Irun was heard. Clausel, after having ordered the 50th of Maransin's division to ascend the Rhune, hurried off to the col[2] between the Rhune and the Ibantelly over which passes the track from

---

1. Lapene, *Campagne de* 1813—1814. He commanded the battery of Taupin's division.

2. This is sometimes called the Col de Vera, but in all the reports of the period the term Puerto or Col de Vera refers to that by which the road from St. Jean de Luz by Olhette crosses the hills above Vera. In those days it was the principal road between France and Spain in that area. The present road by the pass of Ibardin was not made until 1893.

Sare to Vera. On arriving there he found that a Spanish brigade, which had driven back one of his outposts, was moving as if to ascend the Rhune; he then sent orders that the 32nd (two battalions) of Conroux's division was to occupy the chapel of Olhain hill and the Fagadia rocks in support of the 12th Light already in position on the Soubicia spur above the Col de Vera. Maransin at Sare was also ordered to send the 34th to join the 50th, and to hold the two other regiments of Barbot's brigade in readiness to ascend the Rhune if required. Between the long spur with its three-pronged head which runs down south from the Bayonnette and the ridge to the eastward, over which is carried at the Puerto de Vera the road from Vera to Olhette, lies a deep and thickly wooded ravine through which runs the stream which rises below the Col d'Ibardin and joins the Vera stream to the east of the village. Still more to the east there rises above the Vera-Sare track a high, rounded isolated ridge, which the British soldiers called the *hogsback*, the western end of which approaches the eastern prong of the Bayonnette spur, leaving a gap of a few hundred yards through which passes the road and the ravine stream. So the *hogsback* like a great embankment almost closes the entrance to the ravine. It was held by four companies of the French 31st Light.

To gain entrance to the valley and use the road was the task of Kempt's brigade of the Light Division, therefore the French had to be cleared off the *hogsback* which was necessary also because round its eastern end was the line of advance of Giron's corps; and with this opened the fighting of the day.

The attack on its western end was allotted to five companies of the 3/95th Rifles under Lieut.-Colonel Ross, supported by the 17th Portuguese Regiment, and right well was it done. An eye-witness says:

Never was a movement more beautifully executed, for they walked quietly up and swept them regularly off without firing a shot until the enemy turned their backs, when they served them out with a most destructive discharge. The movement excited the admiration of all who witnessed it.[1]

an opinion endorsed by the approving cheers raised by their comrades of the Light and also by the 4th Division. The eastern end was cleared by a company of the 43rd and a Spanish battalion. When this preliminary was over the general advance took place about 8 a.m.

Kempt's and Longa's right brigades pushed through the gap and into the great ravine, covered by the rifle battalions and Longa's men. The 43rd moved by the road heading for the Puerto de Vera and the French camps on either side of it, the 17th Portuguese advancing between it and the left of Giron's corps.

Let us borrow the description of the fighting in the ravine from an actor in it, the leader of the 43rd, and the great historian of the War.

> Soon the open slopes of the mountains were covered with men and fire; a heavy confused sound of mingled shouts and musketry filled the deep hollows and the white smoke came curling up above the dark forest trees which covered their gloomy recesses. The French, compared with their assailants, seemed few and scattered, and Kempt's brigade soon forced its way without a check through all the retrenchments in the main pass, his skirmishers spreading wider and breaking into small detachments of support as the depth of the ravine lessened and the slopes merged into the higher ridges. Longa's brigade, fighting in the gulf between, seemed labouring and overmatched, but beyond, the riflemen and cacadores of Colborne's brigade were seen coming out in small bodies from a forest which covered the three tongues of land up to the edges of the platform.[2]

---

1. Kincaid, *Adventures in the Rifle Brigade.*
2. Napier, *History of the Peninsular War.*

It is now time to turn to the doings of this brigade. Before doing so it may be well to say something regarding its commander, Lieut.-Colonel John Colborne,[1] and his actions prior to the engagement. There were many good battalion and brigade commanders in Wellington's army, but of these no one perhaps had a higher reputation than he who commanded the 52nd Light Infantry.

In the hard struggles of the Peninsular War his name became so well known and his talents so appreciated, that at the close of it no one, after the great Duke himself, would have been regarded by the army as more fit for the highest commands.[2]

During the short time the camp of his brigade had been near Vera, Colborne was on horseback from morning till night reconnoitring the country over which his brigade would have to act:

. . . . thus when he led the troops into action he knew the ground and was enabled to take advantage of every accidental irregularity that favoured his movement at the moment. He thus inspired the highest confidence in the mind of every officer and soldier whom he led, that whatever they might have to do would be done in the best manner and with the least possible exposure to loss.[3]

On the evening of the 6th October the plan of attack was communicated to the officers commanding companies:

The redoubts were to be carried by repeated charges of the 52nd, whilst the other regiments of the brigade, the 2/95th and 1st and 3rd cacadores were to act as skir-

---

1. Field-Marshal Lord Seaton. An unpublished memoir, the *Oxfordshire Light Infantry Chronicle,* 1904.
2. Lord Seaton. An unpublished memoir, the *Oxfordshire Light Infantry Chronicle,* 1904.
3. Moorsom, *History of 52nd Regiment.*

mishers covering its advance; the irregularities of the hill where the charging column could find shelter to breathe between the attacks were distinctly pointed out to the officers. The men requested permission to leave their knapsacks in the bivouacs and this was granted.

At 8 a.m. on the 7th Colborne's brigade skirted the left of the village and formed for action. The deep ravine already mentioned separated it from Kempt's brigade, and each had to fight its way independently to the summit of the French positions. The rifle battalions advanced extending so as to cover the whole front of the three prongs of the Bayonnette spur, the 2/95th the left prong and the 1st and 3rd cacadores. the centre and right, with Longa's left brigade on the extreme left rear. The 52nd took the centre prong. From the village the climb up these spurs is a stiff one and the gorges between them are thickly wooded.

Gradually the extended rifle battalions, driving back the French posts swarmed round the star redoubt, which stands at a point where the prongs diverge from the main spur, as if to storm it. The French sallying forth from it drove them back on all sides; the 52nd was not in sight for the ascent is steep and wooded to within about 300 yards of the redoubt, whence there is an open, gentle upward slope. Just then the 52nd appeared, so far the men had to scramble up almost singly, but five companies had now formed up and the sixth was forming. Led by Colborne the five companies charged the French and drove them back into the redoubt. Napier thus describes the scene as viewed from the other side of the great ravine:

> When about half-way up (towards the Puerto de Vera) an open plateau gave a clear view over the Bayonnette slopes and all eyes were turned that way. On the broad open space in front of the star fort the cacadores and riflemen of Colborne's brigade were seen coming out in small bodies from a forest which covered the three

tongues of land up to the edge of the platform. Their fire was sharp and pace rapid and in a few minutes they closed in on the redoubt as if resolved to storm it, the 52nd were not then in sight, and the French, thinking from the dark clothing all were Portuguese, rushed in close order out of the entrenchment; they were numerous and very sudden, and this rough charge sent their scattered assailants over the rocky edge of the descent. With shrill cries the French followed; but just then the 52nd, partly in line, partly in column, appeared on the platform, and raising their shout rushed forward. The red uniform and the full career of the regiment startled the hitherto adventurous French, they stopped short, wavered and turning fled to the entrenchment; the 52nd following hard entered the works with them, the riflemen and cacadores, who had meanwhile rallied, passed it on both flanks, and for a few moments everything was hidden by a dense volume of smoke. Soon, however, the British shout pealed again and the whole mass emerged on the other side, the French now the fewer flying, the others pursuing until the second entrenchment half-way up the parent slope enabled the retreating troops to make another stand. The exulting and approving cheers of Kempt's brigade now echoed along the mountain-side and with renewed vigour the men continued to scale the craggy mountain, fighting their toilsome way to the top of the Puerto ('de Vera').

To return to Colborne's brigade, after a pause of a few minutes to give the men breath, the attack was resumed according to the original plan and each redoubt captured in succession. On arrival at the last, a redoubt and an entrenchment along the top of the main range, an ineffectual resistance was made by the French holding it, and they soon fled, leaving three mountain guns in the hands of the brigade. The pursuit was continued down the reverse (northern) slopes of the mountain where 22 officers and nearly 400 men surrendered to a part of the 52nd led on by Colborne.[1]

Longa's brigade on the extreme left advanced so slowly that it failed entirely to threaten the enemy's right flank or entrenchments. The French speedy retreat from the Bayonnette redoubt and works on the hill-top was doubtless due to the facts that their line of retreat towards Ascain was now about to be cut off by the advance of Freyre's Spaniards from the Col du Pourier towards Joliment, and that any movement towards their left was barred by Kempt's brigade which, having gained the Puerto, was now moving westwards along the ridge, so nothing remained but to hurry down the northern slopes of the Bayonnette. Fortunately for them a brigade of Villatte's reserve division had advanced from Serres and having checked Freyre's advance towards Ascain, was able to rally the remnants of Bechaud's brigade.

While all this was going on, Giron's Spaniards and the 17th Portuguese had also been successful. After the capture of the *hogsback*, his columns had fought their way up the wooded bank to the right of the Puerto de Vera; on reaching the summit the left column was held up by a strong abattis and the fire of the French 70th; encouraged however, as Napier says, by the dash and spirit of a young British officer, one of Alten's A.D.C.'s, the 70th was driven back on to the Soubicia spur; the 88th finding itself unsupported, retired to the upper slopes of the Rhune, where the 70th eventually joined it.

Clausel had all along been anxious about the safety of Taupin's division if attacked, owing to its separation from

1. Napier says that the surrender was due to Colborne, his staff and a few men crossing their march unexpectedly. The unpublished memoir already quoted says: "Their capture was in truth the result of foresight and good management. It was a regular chase, the 52nd keeping to the high ground above the valley which the French descended, and when he (Colborne) summoned them to surrender the leading companies were but a few yards behind." The memoir is believed to have been written by two officers of the regiment, one of whom (at least) was present.

the other divisions of his corps by the mass of the Grande Rhune, and had informed Soult of his anxiety, pointing out that owing to the conformation of the ground it would be impossible to reinforce Taupin in time were he attacked by very superior forces, as was likely; the warning does not appear to have had any effect.

As soon as Clausel learnt that both the Bayonnette and the Puerto de Vera were in possession of the enemy, he realized that everything possible must now be done to safeguard his possession of the Grande Rhune. He had already, as we have seen, eight battalions on or about the mountain, and now sent to their support General Barbot and the three remaining battalions of his brigade with orders to occupy the Petite Rhune.

The fighting ceased about midday; about 4 p.m., however, three of Giron's battalions drove the 32nd from the Fagadia rocks and attempted unsuccessfully to scale the rocks below the summit of the Rhune held by the French 12th Light, the firing going on till after dark.

Soon after 7 a.m. on the 7th the 6th Division began the demonstration ordered against the French left held by D'Erlon's corps. Of this corps, Darmagnac's division was in first line about Ainhoa with advanced posts holding the ironworks of Urdax, about 2 miles north of the village of that name, the heights above the village on both sides of the Col de Maya-Ainhoa road, and on their extreme right rear a loopholed house—the Maison Poncagaray on the left bank of the Nivelle. Abbe's division was at Souraide and Darricau's several miles away at the camp of Ibarron. The troops employed were the Portuguese brigade, commanded by Colonel Douglas; by 9 a.m. the French had been driven from the ironworks, the heights and the loop-holed house. But now Douglas seems to have pushed his advance to his left front and too far; for D'Erlon, judging from Douglas's movements that he either intended to turn Darmagnac's right or to join hands with the brigade of the 7th Division in front of Zugaramurdi, which was in close touch with Clausel's outposts in that direction, and threatening the Granada redoubt, sent down Abbe's division to attack Douglas's flank. This move obliged him to retire, having lost 150 men. The demonstration, however, fulfilled its object; though it entailed on Douglas a severe censure from the Commander of the Forces. Ever mindful of the fighting strength and moral of his army, Wellington's anger was always excited by unnecessary casualties. On the 10th October he wrote to General Colville, as follows:

> I am sorry to be obliged to express my disapprobation of the conduct of an Officer (Col. Douglas) of whom I have always entertained a good opinion; but I must say that it is unworthy of one of his reputation to get his brigade into scrapes for the sake of a little *gloriole* of driving in a few piquets, knowing, as he must do, that it is not intended he should engage in a serious affair; and that, whenever he becomes engaged with a body of any strength, to retreat with honour is difficult, and without loss is impossible. He must observe that if the enemy's troops were ten times more disheartened than they are, his conduct in getting his brigade into unnecessary scrapes would make soldiers of them again, and if the Portuguese were better soldiers even than they are, they would become worse from the same conduct."[1]

In the Peninsular Army the highest standard of credit was when a brilliant deed was done with little loss.[2]

Early on the 8th Wellington went to Vera and towards Sare to arrange measures for the expulsion of the French from the Great Rhune. Owing to one of those mists, which are so frequent over the western end of the Pyrenees, he was unable for some time to reconnoitre the approaches to the mountain; when it cleared away he "found the mountain to be least inaccessible by its right (i.e. on its eastward side), and that the attack on it might be connected with advantage with an attack on the

---

1. Wellington to Colville, 10th October, 1813.
2. Kincaid, *Random Shots from a Rifleman*.

enemy's works in front of the camp of Sare."[1] He accordingly ordered Giron's corps to concentrate towards their right.

At 4 p.m. the Spaniards, backed up by some companies of the 2/95th Rifles,[2] attacked and drove the French from the Bechinen rocks and the Olhain Chapel hill, whilst detachments of the 7th Division from the pass of Echalar menaced the French redoubts and entrenchments which covered Sare, and the 6th Division demonstrated as if intending to turn Clausel's left by advancing towards Amots.

Clausel, alarmed by these events and fearing lest he should be cut off from Sare, abandoned the lower slopes of the Rhune and the Ste. Barbe redoubt,[3] which covered the camp to the south, and also commanded the roads to Sare from Vera and the pass of Echalar. The way being thus cleared Giron sent the battalion of Las Ordenes to occupy some rocks close up to the summit of the Rhune.

Owing to Clausel's abandonment of his advanced line, the continual musketry fire about Sare and his isolated position, the Officer commanding the 12th Light, whose morale was shaken by the events of the last two days, after dark took counsel of his fears lest a further advance by the enemy would cut off the only line of retreat open to him, the spur which falls down towards the Col de Sare on the Sare-Ascain road. He communicated his fears to the Officer commanding the 34th, and, on the latter agreeing with him, both regiments evacuated the summit of the Rhune and moved down to the Petite Rhune, without obtaining permission to do so from the higher command. An officer was, however, sent to report the movement.

This officer reached corps headquarters at about 11 p.m. On receiving the report Clausel's first intention was to send up orders to these regiments to resume their positions on the

---

1. Wellington's Dispatch, 9th October, 1813.
2. Kincaid, *Adventures in the Rifle Brigade.*
3. The Ste. Barbe redoubt, which is about a mile to the south of Sare, stands on the northern end of a detached ridge below which pass, one on each side, the roads from Vera and Echalar.

Great Rhune, but:

> . . . . the officer who had been sent assured me that the
> Colonel, to whom I had given detailed orders, had only
> decided to make this movement when he saw he could
> only retreat as long as the col on the Ascain-Sare road was
> free. I was wrong to believe it, and in not sending a posi-
> tive order to resume their positions on the Rhune.[1]

On the night of the 8th Conroux's and Maransin's divisions resumed their positions on the high ground to the north
of Sare with their right on the Petite Rhune and outposts in
the village.

On the morning of the 9th the Spaniards moved up and
occupied the summit of the Rhune, and the Light Division
encamped on the spur to the east of the Puerto de Vera. The
7th Division continued its demonstrations in front of Sare
and the Granada redoubt; one party getting too closely engaged on the outskirts of the village were hardly treated by
the French and would have suffered more had not some of
Giron's Spaniards come to their assistance.[2] The 6th Division
also showed troops and D'Erlon reported that an attack on his
section appeared to be imminent. To further safeguard his position at Sare, Clausel ordered the roads at Hembiscay—about
half a mile south of Sare—to be barricaded, and a line of
trenches to be dug covering the village to the south.[3]

Throughout the three days' fighting both Freyre's and Giron's Spanish divisions had behaved exceedingly well, and Wellington in his dispatch gave them due credit.[4] He said Freyre's:

> . . . . troops behaved admirably and turned and carried
> the enemy's entrenchment on the hill (Mandale), with
> great dexterity and gallantry, and it gives me singular

---

1. Clausel's report to Soult, 18th October, 1813.
2. Wellington to Hope, Lesaca, 7.30 a.m., 10th October.
3. Commandant Burel's report, Sare, 9th October.
4. Wellington to Bathurst, Lesaca, 9th October, 1813.

satisfaction to report the good conduct of the officers and troops of the Reserve of Andalusia as well in the operations of the 7th as in those of yesterday. The attack made yesterday by the battalion of Las Ordenes under the command of Colonel Hore was made in as good order and with as much spirit as I have seen made by any troops, and I am much satisfied with the spirit and discipline of the whole of this corps; and I cannot applaud too highly the execution of the arrangements for these attacks by the Mariscal del Campo Don. P. Giron, and the General and Staff Officers under his direction.

After the operations from the 7th to 9th October, both sides retained the positions they had either gained or retreated to, and commenced to dig themselves in on the ground occupied. A few days later, however, Soult visited Clausel's corps and ordered him to retake the Ste. Barbe redoubt by a night attack. This was made by three battalions of Conroux's division and a sapper company on the night 12th/13th October; the Spanish garrison being surprised[1] were driven out with a loss of over 200 men, of whom 174 were made prisoners. Two attempts to retake the redoubt were made by the Spaniards early in the morning of the 13th, but both failed; and the French advance obliged the Allies to evacuate all their advanced posts to the south of Sare. After visiting the ground, Wellington ordered that no further attempt was to be made to regain the redoubt. It was, he said, farther to the front of the line held than he thought it was when he ordered it to be occupied, and was so close to the houses of Sare that it invited a surprise attack.[2]

During these days Foy on the extreme French left at St. Jean Pied-de-Port made no move.

---

1. *Larpent's Journal.* "The day before this surprise, the Officers at General Cole's were remarking that it was surprising the Spaniards kept the redoubt and their post, for their officers were never seen there with their men to keep them on the alert, and the men were cooking without their arms within twenty yards of the French sentries quite unconcerned."
2. Wellington to Bathurst, 18th October, 1813.

CHAPTER 11

Objectives Achieved

On the allied side the leading of the troops had everywhere been good, notwithstanding the difficulties of the ground. The engagements recorded had proceeded strictly according to the plan outlined in the orders. The allied army had everywhere been successful, and on the 9th October Wellington was in possession of all the country within French territory he had set himself to gain.

To what did he owe his success? Was it due mainly to the fighting qualities of his subordinate commanders and the soldiers of his army? How well they fought their deeds proclaim. It may not be out of place to quote what Napier, an eye-witness, says.

Surely the bravery of troops who assailed and carried such stupendous positions must be admired. Day by day for more than a month entrenchment had risen over entrenchment, covering the vast slopes which were scarcely accessible from their natural steepness and asperity. This they could see, yet cared neither for the growing strength, the height of the mountains nor the breadth of the river and its mighty rushing tide: all were despised and they marched with this confident valour.[1]

---

1. Another witness, Colonel Frazer, R.H.A., letter of 9 p.m., 8th October. "We returned to our horses and turned over the mountains to look at the batteries and entrenchments carried the day before by the Light Division. It is not easy to imagine a stronger natural position, strengthened as it was by redoubts, by abattis and entrenchments on every knoll with paths, where there were any at

The difficulties of the ground, in some places as enclosed as in England, the height and steepness of the mountains, densely wooded in many parts, must have made the formation of plans by subordinate leaders anxious work. Without this confidence and bravery the successes could not have been won. But the key of victory lay in the Commander's plan, and a truly audacious one it was, but Wellington took no counsel of his fears "as to what might happen if things went ill with his left wing and a rushing sixteen-feet tide in a few hours cut off their retreat."

It was, as Napier says, "a general's, not a soldier's battle." In every difficulty the plan came to the help of the lesser commanders. Surprise found the enemy's commander out of his place, and he and his army unprepared. At every point attacked the enemy was assailed in overwhelming force, and out of the plan proceeded the fact that whenever flanking assistance was needed it came into force almost automatically.

The front covered by Reille's and Clausel's corps from the sea to Sare was about 12 miles. When the action commenced the first line was held by no more than 12,000 men. As local reserve Reille had 5,070 men, of whom not more than half were immediately available, owing to Boyer's second brigade having gone to work on the Ciboure defences, which are about 5 miles from the river-crossing at Behobie. Clausel had about 8,300, at least half of whom were required to defend the camp at Sare and the roads thence to Ascain and St. Pée. The general reserve, Villatte's division, less one brigade at Cambo, about 7,000 strong, was in three groups, one brigade which Soult brought up to Urrugne, one at Ascain and one at Serres.

---

all, scarcely practicable." 13th October. "Having again examined the position from which the enemy was driven on the 7th, I am the more surprised they should have been forced. It is a toil to get up to most of their entrenchments even without arms to carry and anybody to meet at the top: but bravery will, generally speaking, do anything and everything." To anyone who has been over the ground, the above, and Napier's words, will not appear exaggerated.

On the 7th October the allies attacked Reille's front with 25,000 men, and 3,500 in reserve; Clausel's front with 16,700 and 5,700 in reserve. On that day the allies brought into action, exclusive of reserves, 42,500 men against 20,800 French infantry engaged out of a total of 55,600 infantry under Soult's command.[1]

A French writer[2] commenting on these operations, says:

> Wellington played a sure game, and had the means whereby events shaped themselves as he intended. It is amazing that English sycophants should hold up as a genius one who had need of such helps, and who, when at equal strength with his enemy, continually said his strength was not sufficient.

Perhaps unfortunately, the critic a few pages later on quotes the dictum of Napoleon that "the science of war consists of fighting with two against one."

On the French side the surprise was complete. On the 6th October Soult had inspected the divisions of D'Erlon's corps, that night he slept at Espelette, intending to visit Clausel's corps on the 7th. At 7 a.m. on that day he was at Ainhoa, confident that the allied attack, which he daily expected, would be against his left wing. Hearing the gunfire in the direction of Irun, and recognizing that the movement of the 6th Division brigade against the village was only a demonstration, he hurried off to gain the right of his army, where he arrived about 1 p.m., when the fighting there had ceased. There does not appear to be any record of the route he took, of the generals he saw, or of any orders he gave during his journey. Had he stopped at some central place such as Ascain or Serres, he could have been in touch with both flanks and might have taken up control of the operations. As he did not do so, the superior command of the army had no influence or control throughout the day, and virtually disappeared. Consequently the subordinate chiefs

---

[1] Includes Paris's brigade of the army of Aragon about 2,500 strong.

[2] Commandant Clerc, *Campagne du Maréchal Soult dans les Pyrenees Occidentales.*

were left to act on their own, and they, having as much as they could do to maintain their positions, had neither the time nor opportunity for mutual co-operation. Nor did they receive any assistance from the general reserve.

Taupin's division of Clausel's corps held the Col de Vera and the Bayonnette mountain, which is a continuation east-wards of the Mandale, and rises some 2,000 feet above the valley of Vera and the low ground between Olhette and Ur-rugne. He was isolated from the rest of the corps by the massif of the Great Rhune. This isolation had been pointed out to Soult by Clausel. He said:

> Your Excellency knows I cannot send him any rein-forcements from Sare, because of the distance and the difficulties of the ground. From Sare it would take the head of a column a whole day's march to reach the Bayonnette. Moreover, if I detached brigades it would unduly weaken the centre of the army.

He predicted that, if attacked, "Soult's defence would fail and his retreat be very difficult." Soult appears to have paid no attention to the warning.[1]

Taupin's orders were that if obliged to retreat he was to do so towards Ascain, that is by the northern slopes of the mountains. It was only from this side that assistance could reach him, and it was only the general reserve which could supply it. This reserve, less the Spanish brigade at Cambo, was about 7,000 strong, had two brigades at Ascain and one at Serres. So placed, the division could reinforce Clau-sel fairly quickly, from Ascain to Sare being 3 miles, and from Serres 4 miles over a not very hilly track. It would seem that this was the purpose of its position, bearing in mind Soult's belief that his left would be attacked. From his report to the War Minister, however, it would appear that this was not the case, for he says [2] "the reserve division had

1. Clausel to Soult, 26th September, 1813.
2. Soult to Guerre, 18th October, 1813.

orders to move rapidly to the ridge which extends from Olhette to support the troops holding the Bayonnette and the line of the Bidassoa." At 9 a.m. on the 7th October, Villatte received the order to move. Starting at this hour it was impossible to reach either the Bayonnette or the line of the Bidassoa.[1]

All that Villatte could do was with one brigade to check the advance of Freyre's towards Ascain, and so cover the retreat of the units of Taupin's division; and with the other two brigades to hold the high ground south of Urrugne.

Wellington's simultaneous attack on the French front held every section of it strongly engaged. None could assist his neighbour, and all needed it. Help could only come from local reserves and the general reserve, and these did not exist or were too far away to render it in time. The first line broken, all the reserves could do was to hold points on which it could be rallied, and this only because the allied commander ceased his advance.

Captain Vidal de la Blache considers that D'Erlon cannot escape censure for allowing his three divisions to become "immobilized" owing to the demonstration made by the 6th Division. He is of opinion that had D'Erlon shown more energy—presumably by strongly reinforcing Clausel or attacking himself—it would have been possible for Clausel to have withdrawn all Conroux's division from Sare and placed it on the Rhune, which could then have been held.

This might or might not have been the case. Clausel had already eleven battalions on the mountain, four of Conroux's, five of Maransin's, and two of Taupin's divisions. Room might have been found perhaps for Conroux's five battalions; but without substantial assistance from D'Erlon only Rouget's brigade of Maransin's division would have been left to hold the Sare defences.

---

1. Clerc: "There is not an officer acquainted with the country who will not recognize that Villatte was absolutely 'hors de portee pour soutenir leu troupes a la Bayonnette.'"

But there is another side to the question. The road from Spain by the Baztan valley and the pass of Maya bifurcates on French territory being reached at the Urdax ironworks; one branch follows the course of the Nivelle towards the bridge of Amots, being joined near there by the road from Sare to St. Pée, and thence goes northwards by Arcangues to Bayonne. The other branch passes by Ainhoa, Souraide and Ustaritz to Bayonne, with an off shoot leading from Ainhoa to Espelette, Cambo and the River Nive. If D'Erlon lost his position the gap of Amots was opened, Clausel's flank and that of the rest of the French Army could be turned, and two almost direct lines of advance on Bayonne secured to the allies.

Had D'Erlon moved any considerable part of his force to aid Clausel, what would the general commanding the 6th Division have done? His instructions were "to make some demonstration to help the enemy in uncertainty and prevent his detaching any considerable part of his force from the position he occupies near Ainhoa." These seem to permit, if not require, active interference if demonstrations were insufficient. Had he done so, and attacked, the 3rd Division on his left, whose advanced brigade was in actual touch with the enemy in front of Zugaramurdi,[1] and the 7th Division also, would certainly have become engaged, and the 4th Division, which had not been called on to assist the Light, was only about 4 miles distant.

Though contrary to Wellington's plans and wishes, events might have caused the battle of the Nivelle to have been fought on the 7th October instead of on the 10th November.

The possibility of this happening may perhaps have been considered by Wellington, but, possessing as he did the gift of accurately gauging the characters of the generals opposed to him, he probably considered a demonstration would be quite

---

1. Journal of a commissariat officer (3rd Division), 1st September, 1813. "This morning we camped on heights of Zugaramurdi—our piquets extending down the mountain into the woods in face of the enemy's position on the frontier."

sufficient to tie D'Erlon to his position, for he had ample grounds for judging D'Erlon to be the most cautious and unenterprising of Soult's corps commanders.

The impression made on Soult by the events of the 7th and 9th October may be gathered from the following extracts from letters and orders issued by him on the evening of the 7th. To Thouvenot, Governor of Bayonne, he wrote:

> Events to-morrow will probably be more serious. I again desire you to press on with all your strength the works of the entrenched camp of Bayonne, and also those commanding the roads which are very important. Everybody on them, even the bourgeoisie, and, if necessary, by night as well as by day.

Thouvenot was also ordered to arm all the conscripts at Bayonne, and set them to work on the defences. The cavalry divisions of P. Soult and Treilhard were ordered to move up to the neighbourhood of Bayonne, and a battalion from its garrison with a number of national guards was sent to Cambo to work on the bridge-head defences which were as yet unfinished.

On the army and the public the effects were disastrous. Writing to the Minister of War,[1] his A.D.C., Major Balthazar, said:

> I regret to have to repeat what I wrote some little time back; the army could not have less confidence in itself. It is a distressing thing to see everyone persuaded we are going to be beaten.... I can see clearly from the Marshal's dispositions what his plans are in case of retreat, and retreat is more than probable. D'Erlon will retreat on Cambo, where the bridge is not yet completed; and he (the Marshal) on Bayonne, where the entrenched camp works are equally unfinished.

The diminishing moral of the French was accompanied by further loss of discipline. At Urrugne, Ascain and Sare the

---

1. Balthazar to Guerre, 8th October, 1813.

houses and goods of the inhabitants were plundered by the soldiers, who told them it was better that their property should be taken by their own countrymen than by the enemy; similar outrages took place behind the army at Arcangues and St. Pée. Soult did all he could to stop this plundering. A captain of the 45th Regiment, a chevalier of the Legion of Honour, who encouraged his company to loot a house and assaulted a gendarme who was trying to prevent it, was tried by court martial, sentenced to death, and was shot.

Unfortunately it was not the French soldiers only who plundered, many of the allied army did the same. Writing to Sir John Hope on the 8th October, Wellington said:

I have sad accounts of the plunder by soldiers yesterday, and I propose again to call the attention of the officers to the subject. I saw yesterday many men coming in from Urrugne loaded with plunder. If we were five times as strong as we are, we could not venture to enter France if we cannot prevent our soldiers from plundering.

The same day he issued the following General Order.

The Commander of the Forces is concerned to be under the necessity of republishing his orders of 9th July last, as they have been unattended to by the officers and troops who entered France yesterday. According to all the information he has received, outrages of all description were committed by the troops in the presence even of their officers who took no pains whatever to prevent them.

The Commander of the Forces has already determined that some officers, so grossly negligent of their duties, shall be sent to England, that their names may be brought to the attention of the Prince Regent, and that His Royal Highness may give such directions respecting them as he may think proper, as the Commander of the Forces is determined not to command officers who will not obey his orders.

With the Duke of York at the Horse Guards, it is very probable that after arrival in England the Prince Regent for the King, had no further use for their services.

Wellington's prompt action bore good fruit; for almost certainly to it was due the fact that six weeks later he w; able to report:[1]

> .... a new spirit among the officers to keep their men order .... that the conduct of the Portuguese and British troops has been exactly what I wished, and that the natives of this part of the country are not only reconciled to the invasion, but wish us success, afford us all the supplies in their power, and exert themselves to get information for us.

But meanwhile, the inhabitants, depressed by the defeat; their army had suffered, by the conduct of those who should have protected them and of some of the allied troops, had begun to leave their homes and make their ways into the interior of France. In the army also, there was a sort of general uneasiness regarding the course of events both locally and in Germany. It was not so much fear of invasion as concern regarding what was happening to the French army in Germany, which was heightened by the rumour of a disaster in Saxony which reached Bayonne from Bordeaux on the 16th October.[2]

---

1. Wellington to Bathurst, 21st November, 1813.
2. Thouvenot to Guerre, 14th and 16th October, 1813.

CHAPTER 12

Soult Prepares to Hold

After the failure of his attack on San Marcial on the 31st August, and the surrender of San Sebastian on the 9th September, Soult, though he still carried on his attempts to come to an agreement with Marshal Suchet regarding a combined offensive, must have realized that he would have to remain on the defensive at any rate until his army received reinforcements. It will be remembered that in July, almost immediately after assuming command, he ordered the construction of two entrenched camps for the outside defence of Bayonne, because he rightly judged that the fortress, which was in a bad state of defence, would be the real objective of any forward movement by the enemy. The camps could not be finished and armed for a considerable time, it was essential therefore that other positions in the country between the Bidassoa and Bayonne should be prepared.

Thus the security of Bayonne was the primary cause of his plans for the intermediate positions he contemplated. Having lost his original first line, that of the Bidassoa and the Rhune as held prior to and after the San Marcial attack, he was now obliged to fall back on his second line, its right being at St. Jean de Luz, which was protected by the entrenched camps of Ciboure and Bordegain, which covered the suburb of Ciboure on the left bank of the Nivelle, the main road from Spain and the crossing of the Nivelle by the St. Jean de Luz bridge. From thence the line ran by the ridge which extends from Olhette to the main road, the Petite Rhune, the heights to the north of Sare and Ainhoa, the Atchulegui, Chapora and Mondarrain heights to St. Jean Pied-de-Port.

Behind this second line was to be a third, with its right also at St. Jean de Luz, thence it was to follow the course of the Nivelle to St. Pée. Crossing the Nive at Cambo its left would rest on the Ursouia mountain, thereby covering the main road from St. Jean Pied-de-Port by Urcuray and Mendionde.[1] At Cambo there was to be a double bridge-head armed with 20 guns and sufficiently strong to withstand an *"attaque de vive force."* [2]

Soult from September to November appears to have been seized with, what Vidal de la Blache aptly terms, *"un veritable vertige de terrassements,"* and seems to have so little gauged the character of his opponent as to imagine that the hero of Assaye and many other victories would be intimidated by the piling up of such entrenchments as he proposed.[3] Having occupied his second line, what was Soult to do? The Emperor was silent, the War Minister for political and financial reasons was pressing him to take the offensive again but could promise no reinforcements. Soult, however, took the better view, the Bayonne and other defences were unfinished, and he refused to advance.

Writing to the Minister on 18th October, he thus states his views.

> You will have gathered from my daily reports that I expect a fresh attack by the enemy. I am making the necessary arrangements not only to repulse it with vigour, but also to strengthen the troops in their positions. I have not been intimidated by the enemy's success on 7th October, by his great numerical superiority or by

---

1. The present road in the Nive valley did not then exist.
2. Soult to Guerre, 26th October, 1813.
3. Soult to Guerre, 26th October, 1813; "when the defences of the successive lines are completed, the enemy cannot persist in his idea of attacking."

his offensive demonstrations. In the actual state of affairs I consider I ought to prepare to fight a general action, rather than run the risks of partial fights against positions I can neither carry nor defend if I should regain them. If I received a check in such isolated attacks, I would on the morrow be compelled to cross the Nive, and perhaps even the Adour, because I cannot detach troops from the line held owing to the army being everywhere in close contact with the enemy, and every division has in front of it a force of the enemy stronger than itself. Without doubt the offensive suits us better than the defensive, but to take the offensive implies at least equality in strength with the enemy.

So Soult's decision was to stand and fight in his second position. It will therefore be well to examine this position and its defences more closely.[1] As stated, the line ran from St. Jean de Luz to the Mondarrain mountain, beyond which Foy's division and Paris's brigade held St. Jean Pied-de-Port and various points in the Baigorry valley. The line was divided into three sections, that on the right commanded by Reille extended from the sea at Socoa, by the heights of Bordagain and Ciboure, across the main road at Urtubie, and thence by the ridge of high ground to near the village of Olhette, which lies under the steep northern slopes of the great Rhune, a front of about 3½ miles. The section was divided into two subsections; the northern, termed the camp of Bordagain, was held by Leval's[2] division and comprised all the works connected with the defence of Ciboure and the Bordagain heights. The immediate front of the greater part of this portion was cov-

---

1. With regard to these the details given in Commandant Clerc's *Campagne du Marshal Soult dans les Pyrenees Occidentales* (1894) have been followed. The Commandant whose regiment, the 49th Infantry, formed part of the garrison of Bayonne has made a close examination of the whole area we are concerned with. It was, he says, *"notre terrain de manoeuvres, notre champ d'excursions."*
2. General Leval had replaced General Maucune, who had been transferred to the Army of Italy at Soult's request.

ered by an inundation formed by damming up the Unxain stream where it enters the Bay of St. Jean de Luz near Socoa. Further to the front were the defences about the chapel of Socorry redoubt, and those of the village of Urrugne, which were connected with Socorry by a line of trenches and abattis. The southern section, designated the camp of Urtubie, extended from the main road at the Chateau to near Olhette and comprised a large number of works.

In fact the whole section was covered with redoubts, batteries, defended houses and trenches. Clerc estimates that in the camp of Bordagain there were 3,170 yards of entrenchments to man, which required 4,000 men and 35 guns. In that of Urtubie over 2,000 yards requiring about 3,500 men, without in both cases the provision of any local reserves. With such a mass of works to be garrisoned, Reille calculated that to hold his section 20,000 men, reserves included, were required. As his command did not exceed 11,000 he expostulated with Soult, who decided that the main defence of the southern subsection originally designed in three lines should be confined to the rear one, the others being held by outposts only.

In rear of Reille's section were the French and German brigades of Vellatte's reserve division, under the orders of the Commander-in-Chief "to be manoeuvred as a mass on such points as was necessary."[1] The Spanish brigade of this division was on the extreme left towards Ascain keeping connection with Clausel's section. The Italian brigade was at the camp of Serres on the right bank of the Nivelle with Darricau's division.

Clausel's section in the centre extended from the Little Rhune and its slopes, by the Col St. Ignace along the heights north of Sare as far as the River Nivelle inclusive.

The left section commanded by D'Erlon extended from the river along the heights to the north of Ainhoa, by the Atchulegui and Chapora mountains to the Mondarrain peak.

As Wellington's main attack was made in the area termed

---

1. Order St. Jean de Luz, 28th October, 1813.

the basin of Sare, a brief description of it may be useful before examining the sections held by Clausel and D'Erlon. As the term implies it is an area enclosed by high ground. On the north by the slopes of the Rhune mountain, the heights to the north of Sare and those to the north of Ainhoa. On the east by the Atchulegui, Chapora and Mondarrain mountains (2,460 ft.), which are an extension of the Hausa range, the eastern boundary of the Maya valley. On the south by the range of heights which extend from the Ibantelly peak (2,300 ft.), by the Atchuria mountain (2,480 ft.), to the heights above Zugaramurdi and Urdax. On the west by the southern slopes of the Rhune and by the Ibantelly.

Cut up by minor ridges, offshoots of the mountains, and running generally northwards, the intervening valleys carry off the waters from the surrounding heights, which, after various junctions of streams, eventually join the main stream of the Nivelle, which has its sources below the Mondarrain mountain and in the valleys to the north and west of the Col de Maya. The low country, with the exception of the tops of the ridges, is now generally under cultivation or grassland, is mostly enclosed and there is a good deal of wood. Though there are now many more houses and farms than in 1813, the general aspect of the country is probably not much changed.

Though surrounded by high ground there are various exits and entrances to the basin. Across the pass of Maya runs the main road from Pamplona and the Baztan valley to Ainhoa, Espelette, Cambo and eventually to Bayonne. The pass of Echalar, 1,435 feet, opens a way to that place and the Bidassoa valley; and the col between the Ibantelly mountain and southern slope of the Rhune to Vera and its valley. But the most important in connection with our subject is the gap of Amots, where the River Nivelle has forced its way through the heights which bound the area on the north, leaving space not only for its channel which is deep, but also for an almost level road from below Sare to St. Pée. The southern slopes of these heights to the north of the river are steep and carry a good deal of wood, their lower parts being mostly cultivated with hedged fields, as was probably the case in 1813, but on their northern side the ridges stretch away in long and gently falling spurs of open and uninhabited country, covered with heather and low gorse, till they descend steeply into the open river valley. To the south of the gap the ridge is quite narrow, steep slopes to north and south, the summit open country with heather and gorse and a good deal of wood at the foot of the southern slopes. In the centre of the gap is the old narrow stone bridge of Amots.

In 1813 the existing roads were probably nothing more than cart and mule tracks. "At that time," says Commandant Clerc, "the country was almost impracticable."

Except when in full flood the Nivelle is everywhere fordable to some distance below Amots; at St. Pee it is not fordable, but in this neighbourhood there were three bridges: one a stone bridge near the village Olha about half a mile above St. Pée where the road from Sare crosses the river; a wooden bridge at Urgury, half a mile below St. Pée, and a stone bridge at Harosteguia, a mile and a half below St. Pée. Between St. Pée and Ascain there were fords opposite the village of Helbarron. At Ascain was a stone bridge; as the tide reaches Ascain, the river below that village is only fordable in some places at dead low water. The bridge at St. Jean de Luz was a wooden one in two parts connecting an island in the river with both banks; about a mile above this one the French had thrown a trestle bridge across the river. Near Dorria about a mile below the bridge of Ascain was a bridge of boats to facilitate the movements of the troops holding the Serres defences.

As has been stated, Clausel's section extended from the Little Rhune by the Col de St. Ignace and the heights to the north of Sare to the Nivelle. The summit of the Little Rhune lies parallel to that of the Greater at a distance of about 800 yards, but is nearly 1,000 feet lower. Napier's description of it as a hog's back is apt and accurate; along the spine is an outcrop of jagged rocks. Its southern slope into the valley between the two summits is steep, that on the north is more gradual and crossing a little valley ends in rounded and almost level plateau, the general height of which is about 200 feet below the summit. The western end of the valley between the two summits is closed by a spur from the Great Rhune and the head of a deep depression in which flows the Uharte stream, the source of which is a flat of marshy ground below the spur. At the eastern end of the summit the ground slopes steeply down to the Col de St. Ignace with a deep depression between the two spurs; all the slopes of both Rhunes are covered with long grass and bracken with outcrops of rock here and there. There is not a tree to be seen until the lower ground is reached.[1]

The Lesser Rhune area was held by four battalions of Barbot's brigade of Maransin's division under the command of General Barbot, and much work had been done to strengthen the position since the 8th October. The narrow rocky crest had been turned into series of small works by using the rocks to make walls and passages from near its lowest point above the marsh to its highest where the rocks had been turned into a little citadel termed the Donjon. On the Mouiz plateau a large star redoubt had been built in dry stone; this has no ditch, the walls being from 5 to 7 feet high with a low interior wall as a banquette. This work was connected with the Donjon, a distance of about 350 yards, by an earthen traverse across the little valley with a redan in the lowest part of the ground. On the western edge of the plateau were stone breastworks and trenches commanding the valley and the Uharte stream depression. These works were manned as follows. Two companies of the 4th Light held the star redoubt, two companies the breastworks and the Mouiz side of the traverse with the remaining two companies in reserve. The remainder of the traverse and the defences of the small Rhune were held by

1. Since above was written the valley between the summits is being planted with young trees. The Mouiz redoubt stands today exactly as it was built in 1813.

113

the two battalions of the 40th Line who had also two companies holding a rocky post at the eastern end of the valley between the two Rhunes.

The remainder of Clausel's position ran along the high ground which extends from the Col de St. Ignace to the Nivelle. At their western end above the col these heights rise to about 900 feet, the highest point, 990 feet, being the hill on which stands the signal redoubt, thence they fall gradually to the Col de Mendionde about 650 feet, rise again to over 700 feet at a spur on which is the Louis XVI redoubt and fall gradually to about 500 feet above the river. The defences on this portion of Clausel's section were as follows. On the high ground immediately above the Col de St. Ignace and the deep valley of the stream which has its head there, were two closed redoubts, each for half a battalion and 3 guns with trenches on the slopes below. About a mile to the north of these on the highest point of the long spur which runs towards Serres was another unfinished redoubt, which was held by Darricau's division; its object being to prevent the enemy from passing by the Nivelle valley between Serres and Clausel's right flank. On the highest point of the ridge, 990 feet, was the signal redoubt, a large closed work; on the spur to the east of the Col de Mendionde was the Louis XIV redoubt, 760 feet, for one battalion. On the left rear of this, on the high ground overlooking the Nivelle valley and the bridge of Amots, was the Ste. Madeleine redoubt for one battalion and emplacements for two batteries commanding the bridge and the Sare-St. Pée road. The wooded ground below these redoubts had been formed into a vast abattis, and on the slopes between the redoubt and the abattis were long trenches.

Nearly 2 miles in front of this, the main position, were the redoubts of Ste. Barbe and Granada, placed so as to command the tracks from Vera and the pass of Echalar, each for 200 men and 2 guns, palisaded ditches and surrounded by abattis. Between these redoubts and Sare were lines of trenches covering the village.

All these redoubts, as well as those on D'Erlon's position, are much of the same pattern, square and closed with rampart and ditch: the larger ones about 80 yards square, the sides broken with a small redan for flank defence of the ditches. In his report on the action Clausel states that the Louis XIV and the Madeleine redoubts were unfinished and not in a state of defence and the abattis not completed. From what is left of the Louis XIV it must have been a formidable work, the ditch is still deep and scarped and its rampart still a fair height, and it is so with most of the others.

To the right rear of Clausel's position Darricau's division and the Italian brigade of the Reserve division occupied the camp of Serres on the right bank of the Nivelle, where the old defences of the Revolutionary wars had been repaired, as a support to Clausel. To cover the bridges and Dorria and Ascain one brigade of Darricau's force held the heights on the left bank above these villages.

The main position held by D'Erlon's corps—he had now only two divisions owing to the detachment of Darricau to Serres—was on the high ground to the north of Ainhoa, extending from the Nivelle at the bridge of Amots to its' junction with the Atchulegui mountain at the Col of Finodetta, a distance of about 2½-miles. As stated, these heights differ essentially from those in Clausel's position, being a long narrow ridge, the top of which seldom exceeds more than 100 yards in width, both its northern and southern slopes fall steeply into deep ravines, in which flow streams which join the Nivelle below and above the bridge. These slopes are covered with grass, patches of gorse—an almost impassable obstacle—and bracken, with a good deal of wood. Near the centre of the ridge is a depression, the Col de Harismendia—over which passes a track from Ainhoa to join the Souraide-St. Pée road. Rising steeply from a strip of meadow land on the right bank of the Nivelle, the general height of the western portion is between 600 and 700 feet, whilst that part to the east of the col rises to over 900 feet and falls from thence to 590 at the Col de Finodetta.

The defences on the hill consisted of redoubts on the crest and trenches on the southern slopes. On the extreme western end a small work commanded the river and the bridge below; a larger one at point 669 commanded the river and the approaches to the bridge from the south. Near point 763 were two redoubts close together to the west of and commanding the Harismendia col. Between the 669 redoubt and those of about point 763 was a hutted camp. To the east of the col about point 888 were two redoubts, and beyond these about point 914 was a large open work armed with heavy naval guns.

As the corps had been on the ground since the 10th August the works were in a more advanced state than those in Clausel's section, the ditches appear to have been deeper, the ramparts higher and a greater use made of trenches on the southern slopes, at the foot of which skirmishers had shelter in woods, hedges and cottages. D'Erlon's two divisions had not been seriously engaged in any of the autumn fighting, and the spirit of the troops was more satisfactory than in other divisions of the army.

As it was possible for a force holding the Maya heights to completely turn this position by an advance along the *"chemin des Anglais"* and the Gorospil ridge towards the Mondarrain mountain and Espelette—the route taken by D'Erlon himself when he attacked the Maya pass on the 25th July—the left flank of D'Erlon's position was thrown forward almost at a right angle by the occupation of the Atchulegui, Chapora and Mondarrain heights, and their defence entrusted to Maucomble's brigade of Abbé's division. Owing to supply difficulties the works thrown up were normally held by guards only, the remainder of the brigade being camped between Espelette and the Col de Finodetta. In front of the main position several advanced posts were put in a state of defence in order to delay the enemy's advance.

On the morning of the 10th November the distribution of D'Erlon's corps was as follows. Gruardet's brigade of Darmagnac's division held the western portion of the main division from the Nivelle to the Col de Harismendia. Boivin's brigade of Abbé's division the eastern half; Maucomble's brigade, as stated, the heights on the left flank. In front of the main position Chassé's brigade of Darmagnac's division held the advanced posts, namely the village of Ainhoa, the ironworks, called the forge of Urdax, which commanded the bridge over the Nivelle at Dancharia, a battery at Arbona, which also commanded the bridge, trenches on the right bank, and a loop-holed house with entrenchments on the left bank called "the fortified house" in the British reports.

CHAPTER 13

Wellington's Second Move

Having successfully carried out the first step in an advance into France, Wellington had now to consider how and when his next move was to be made. From his correspondence and other documents available it would seem as if he had by no means made up his mind during the greater part of October.

On the 8th October, Lord Bathurst, referring to the allied operations in Germany, wrote:

> We might expect everything if there were not so many heads against one, and that one Bonaparte. . . . It is impossible to say that a peace, or at least an armistice, may not be suddenly made; but I think things are too complicated to admit of any such event as will at once put Bonaparte at liberty to turn himself against you.

It is almost certain that this letter reached Wellington on the 17th October, because Larpent in his journal states that Major Hare, carrying dispatches and letters up to the 9th October, "fought his way in in the *Landrail*" and dined at Wellington's table on Sunday 17th.[1]

On the 18th Wellington, replying to this letter, wrote:

> I am very doubtful indeed about the advantage of moving any further forward at present. I see that Bonaparte was still at Dresden on 28th (September) and unless

---

1. *Larpent's Journal.*

I could fight a general action against Soult and gain a complete victory, which the nature of the country would scarcely admit of, I should do little good to the allies, should hardly be able to winter in France, and in retiring should probably incur some loss and inconvenience. It is impossible to move our right till Pamplona shall fall, which I think will be within a week,[1] and I will then decide according to the state of affairs at the moment,

and goes on to say that if there was no further movement into France this winter, and he retained command of the Spanish armies, he ought to go into Catalonia to put matters there on a better footing than they are, adding,

How I am to settle the rank and pretensions of the gentlemen left behind I am sure I do not know.[2]

If, however, Wellington was as yet undecided as to his future action, he had firmly made up his mind on two points. The first, as we have seen, that he would make no forward movement until the surrender of Pamplona; the second, that he would not permit even any minor advance by any part of the allied army, lest any such movement should provoke a more or less general action before his own plans were settled. Colville, commanding the 3rd Division, who wished to make a slight advance to his front, was told by the Q.M.G. that "it was not Lord Wellington's intention for the present to push forward the centre of the general line any farther," and on the 15th October a general order was issued that "Neither officers nor men may be allowed to pass the advanced piquets for forage or any other purpose." As has been already stated, he forbade any attempt

---

1. Wellington to Graham, 5th October, 1813. "From what we can make out of an intercepted letter (in cipher) from the Governor of Pamplona, I judge he can hold out till 20th or 25th, and till that time we certainly cannot move our right."

2. Hope was senior as a Lieutenant-General to Beresford, but the latter was a Marshal in the Portuguese service.

being made to retake the Sainte Barbe redoubt in front of Sare. This prohibition does not seem to have extended in practice to Hill's corps on the right from which reconnaissance parties frequently felt the French posts in the Alduides and Baigorry valleys. Here there was little danger of untoward results owing to the isolated position of Foy's division, and such action might alarm Soult as to his left.

During this period both Allies and the French were busy digging themselves in on the positions gained or to which they had retreated after the 7th October. On the allied left this was especially necessary with the Bidassoa and the dangerous estuary so close behind the line held. Numerous redoubts, relics of the Revolutionary War, were repaired and adapted to the existing conditions. Much work was also done along the allied line repairing and improving the so-called roads, especially on that from Vera to Sare[1] in order to facilitate the movement of artillery from the left to the centre of the line.

Wellington also at this time was personally very active, was constantly reconnoitring the French positions from the heights held by his army.[2] From his observation, and also no doubt from those of the Q.M.G. and his staff, the plan of attack on the French position was formed. When it was settled is not clear, but it was before the 25th October, as on that date the Q.M.G. began to send out to the divisional commanders extracts from. . . .

. . . . an Instruction relative to an intended operation in order that you may have an opportunity of examining the ground and considering beforehand the arrange-

---

1. Even to-day there is no real road, nothing but an unmetalled cart track, which in places is by no means easy to follow in the thickly wooded country.
2. Diary of a commissariat officer (3rd Division on heights above Zugaramurdi), 4th November, 1813. "Lord Wellington was about this time constantly occupied in reconnoitring the enemy's fortified position. He was a long time one morning on some rising ground at Zugaramurdi making observations with his glass, which was carried after him by an orderly dragoon."

ments that will be necessary with respect to the disposal of the force which will be under your directions.

The letters issued on the 26th were more definitely worded, in that they stated the Instruction was "for a forward movement intended to be carried out upon the surrender of Pamplona."

This decision does not appear to have been come to on account of any pressure from the Government in England, or by reason of any information he had received regarding the progress of the war in Germany, because it was not till later that he received two most important items of information, namely, the report on the 26th October from "my correspondent in Bayonne,"[1] that they had there no news of Napoleon's army, that it was whispered that it had retired, and that the communication was cut. The other was the important letter from the Prime Minister, Lord Liverpool, of the 20th October, which reached Wellington on the 30th informing him that an arrangement had been concluded between the Austrian and Bavarian governments by which the latter were to take part in the war against France, which arrangement the Prime Minister considered would undoubtedly be carried out unless some unforeseen misfortune happened to the allied forces.

It would seem as if an outside influence over which he had no control, namely the state of the weather, was an important factor leading to Wellington's decision. In the middle of October the weather, which had been fine, began to break, and towards the end of the month had become very stormy and cold. Strong north-easterly winds accompanied by heavy rain and hailstorms had set in, the country was sodden with rain, and the roads, such as they were, broken up and almost impassable. On the heights above Roncevaux the situation became serious. Hope, of the 92nd, in his memoirs thus describes it:

About the middle of October our situation became uncomfortable. The ground was so saturated with moisture that wherever we camped in a day or two our camp

---

1. Wellington to Beresford, Vera, 26th October, 1813.

became a perfect puddle. The weather at last became so very bad, that all the troops on the right of the position were recalled from the heights, except the outlying piquet, and a body of 500 men, called the inlying piquet, to support the others in case of attack. . . . On the 27th snow began to fall, and the wind to whistle, and at daybreak on the 28th the snow was drifted to a considerable depth.

On the morning of the 29th the snow was a foot and a half in the valley where not drifted, but on the hills it was in some places 12 feet in depth. "Part of the outlying piquets were covered and had to be dug out of the snow in a pitiable state."

On the Rhune and its slopes, conditions were also very bad. Simmonds in his diary writes:

It certainly was beginning to be exceedingly cold with frequent storms of hail and rain. Our tents from the tremendous gusts of wind which suddenly and frequently assailed them, were torn and often rendered useless. The Spaniards and Portuguese also lost men from cold and severe weather. Strange to say, in this severe climate exposed to every hardship, not a man was on the sick list in our battalion.

The 4th Division, camped on an exposed spur of the Rhune, were in much the same discomfort.

To maintain the army in its present positions, under conditions such as these, was out of the question. Its strength would be diminished by sickness, its moral lessened, as it was desertions were already very numerous, 500 men deserted in October, and they were not confined to the foreign troops only. The supply of the army was already difficult and would be more so owing to the heavy rain and snow storms in the mountains. Soult himself began to gather comfort from the effect the weather was having on the allied army, he knew all about it from the numerous deserters, for on the 19th October he wrote to Suchet saying, "If I could oblige the enemy's army to remain in their present positions for fifteen days longer it would dissolve *(fondrait)."*

As it was not expedient to maintain the army in its present position it must either advance farther into France or retire across the Spanish frontier. The latter alternative was out of the question. To withdraw into Spain would be to surrender all the advantages gained by the army's successful entry into France. It would be running counter to the wishes of the Government, who looked to Wellington to give a lead to the Northern Powers, would be hurtful to the moral of the army, and certainly create considerable dissatisfaction in Great Britain.[1] The army must therefore advance and attack and Wellington so decided.

Pamplona having surrendered on the 31st October, the whole army, including the blockading force, was now available, and it was now necessary to decide how and when it was to be employed. An attack on Soult's right, if successful, would open the shortest line to Bayonne, have the advantage of the best road in the district, and keep close to the sea the source of supply. But it would involve a considerable concentration towards the allied right, which, under the existing circumstances and close contact of the armies, could hardly be hidden from the enemy. It was also the strongest and best-defended part of the French line; for this reason Wellington "did not deem it expedient to attack it in front." [2]

There remained the centre and left of the French line. An advance from Roncevaux against the enemy's extreme left at St. Jean Pied-de-Port offered undoubted advantages. It would by one move turn the lines of the Nivelle and Nive rivers near

---

1. Graham to Wellington, London, 9th November, 1813. "I most sincerely congratulate you on obtaining Pamplona undamaged. People seem inclined, however, to expect too much as usual, and fancy Bonaparte can never make another stand." The date of the letter in Wellington's dispatches is printed 9th October, an evident misprint, as Graham on 9th October sailed from Passages to England, and Pamplona did not surrender till 31st October.
2. Wellington to Bathurst, St. Pée, 13th November, 1813.

their sources, would give the allies possession of a good road to Bayonne,[1] and would oblige Soult to retire from his present position and either fight a battle in a position near Bayonne, or fall back on that fortress and its entrenched camp and the River Adour. For the reasons already given in connection with the crossing of the Bidassoa, it is not likely that Wellington at this time in any way favoured this movement; he had never, he said in August, "ventured to risk even the communication with the sea," and was not likely to do so now.

It has been considered here because there is on record an undated "memo regarding a forward movement by the right of the army during the winter of 1813 to 1814," which both Captain Vidal de la Blache and Sir John Fortescue consider "can be logically attributed to this period." [2] Briefly the plan outlined was as follows. Hill with the 2nd Division, Morillo and part of Mina's corps with a cavalry regiment and four batteries of artillery, was to advance past St. Jean Pied-de-Port, keeping his columns out of range of the guns of the citadel and detached works, and then take up the best position he could find beyond the town on the road to Bayonne, observing with his right also that leading to Oloron and Pau. The Portuguese Division was to move to St. Etienne de Baigorry, and thence to Anhaux on the Nive "to ascertain what passes there are across the Nive and seize them."

The 3rd Division, with two squadrons of 14th Light Dragoons and a battery, was also to move to St. Etienne, and thence down the Nive to St. Martin d'Arossa and occupy it. The 6th Division to follow the 3rd, and close up to it; the 7th Division was to move to its right and replace the 6th on the Maya, two brigades on the heights and one at Maya, which was to observe the passes from the Baztan valley leading into that of Baigorry. If carried out the scheme involved

---

1. This road from St. Jean Pied-de-Port was by Irissary, Helette and Mendionde; the existing road, which follows closely the course of the Nive, did not then exist.
2. Vidal de la Blache, *L'evacuation de l'Espagne*.

no change in the opposing strength on the allied left, but the centre would be considerably weakened. The infantry strength would be allied about 23,000, of whom 7,500 were Spaniards, and French about 28,000. Wellington probably did not consider this French superiority out of proportion, because as soon as Soult knew of the allied advance and its approximate strength he would necessarily have to reinforce his left, and the means most at hand were the two divisions of D'Erlon's corps.

This scheme has only been examined because of the opinions previously expressed. If, however, one considers the composition of the proposed force, it would seem as if it had been drawn up in September or early October, when the Portuguese Division was in the Alduides valley and the 3rd Division in the Baztan. To carry it out in early November would not have been possible in the severe weather with snow on the mountains; and supply, under the then conditions and at such a distance from the coast, would be extraordinarily difficult. In drawing it up the weather factor does not seem to have been sufficiently considered.

There remains the third alternative; an advance against the French centre and left centre, combined with a demonstration in force against the right. This Wellington decided on at some date prior to the 25th October. It meant a stout fight against a strong position,[1] but he had recognized its weak point, and his plan contained the possibility, if things went well, of a great coup.

An attack having been decided on, it remained to fix the date. No movement from the right could be made until Pamplona surrendered, which took place on the 31st October. Owing to the shortening of the days in November, at that latitude about nine and a half hours, and to increase the chances of surprise, it was desirable that the advance to attack should begin as early in the day as possible. To effect this it was necessary that

1. Rait. *Life of 1st Viscount Gough*. In a letter Gough, then commanding 87th Regiment, wrote: "The French position is strong by nature and made as strong as art could make it."

all the divisions should arrive at their assembly points as nearly simultaneously as possible, and their movements be concealed from the enemy. From the nature of the country and the early commencement of the attack it was inevitable that these preliminary movements must be made before daylight.

Now, the positions of nearly all the attacking divisions were on the heights which extend from the Maya ridge along the heights towards the Ibantelly mountain and the Great Rhune. In nearly every case to gain the lower country they must move by little defined mountain tracks, often through wooded ground, and their difficulties in absolute darkness will be appreciated; but if there was moonlight these would be considerably diminished. The moon was full on 7th November, 1813, and the advance was fixed to commence at daylight on the 8th.

Owing, however, to the effect of heavy rains during the last days of October and the beginning of November on the mountain tracks, Hill's corps would not be able to reach the Baztan valley on the appointed day. On the evening of the 7th November, Wellington wrote to Hope as follows:

I am just returned from the right, there has been much undue rain in that quarter, and the roads are so much destroyed by it that it is quite impossible for the troops to move to-morrow, and probably not next day, our move is therefore deferred till Wednesday (10th).

At this time, and most inopportunely, the Spanish generals appear to have been giving trouble. Freyre, to Wellington's "much concern,"[1] proposed, owing to the wants of his army, to send several of his battalions to the rear to endeavour to provide subsistence for themselves, and Wellington, contrary to his fixed principle of never feeding the Spanish troops,[2] was

---

1. Wellington to Freyre, Vera, 3rd November, 1813.
2. Wellington to Sir J. Murray, Fenada, 6th April, 1813. "In regard to feeding the Spanish troops, I have invariably set my face against it, and have never consented to it, or done it, even for a day, in any instance."

obliged to order the issue to the 4th Spanish Army of 40,000 rations of flour from the British Magazine at Passages.

The case of Giron, commanding the Reserve Army of Andalusia, seems to have been a more serious one, because there is on record an unsigned memo, dated 6th November, of an arrangement for withdrawing this army and sending into cantonments at Yanci in the Bidassoa valley. The reason for the move appears to be unknown. It must have been a very serious and urgent one to make Wellington face the loss of some 8,000 men at such a time. It would almost seem as if the loyalty of these troops was suspected,[1] and this was not the only trouble with Giron. On the evening before the battle, Giron came to Army Headquarters, and demanded ammunition for his corps. Fortunately Colonel Dickson, commanding the artillery, was able to supply what was required; and Wellington sent the following note to Giron at 9 p.m.:

If you had asked for the ammunition on Sunday, I could have given it to you without any inconvenience, because I would have had time to replace it. Now I give it to you, telling you at the same time that if the affair is a hard one the army runs the risk of want of ammunition.

Besides the heavy rains and snow in early November, there was another type of weather which could greatly interfere with the proposed operation, which is the fog and mist which is so frequent over the western end of the Pyrenees. Though usually these fogs come on after midday, yet owing to the amount of rain which had fallen it was not unlikely that on

---

1. In May, 1813, there were rumours in Bordeaux that Ferdinand VII, King of Spain, a prisoner in France, was to be sent back to Spain. Later on, when further details concerning the treaty of Valancay came to be known, Wellington wrote to H. Wellesley: "I am certain that everyone in Spain desires peace, and the soldiers more than others. Here the soldiers know more or less what has happened, but they have not said a word to me. French people have frequently warned me that the Spaniards were meditating treachery." The fact that the Andalusians during movement to the rear were to be shepherded by the 4th British Division seems to add to the suspicion.

the appointed day there would be fogs both on the heights and in the lower country. This had to be provided for, and was so in the final orders. Fortunately the morning of the 10th was both fine and clear.

ACTION TO PREVENT OUTRAGES ON INHABITANTS

As has been stated, many acts of plunder and outrage against the inhabitants of the invaded district of France had been committed by soldiers of the Allied Army after the victory of the 7th October. Moreover, there were officers who had failed to take steps to prevent marauding. Wellington had early in his command recognized how great a factor towards success was conciliatory treatment of the people of the district he was campaigning in, and how derogatory to the honour of the army thefts and outrages were. Before again advancing he determined to make another appeal to the army to respect the persons and properties of the inhabitants. Accordingly the Adjutant-General issued an instruction to general officers commanding corps and divisions on the subject, directing them to assemble commanders of brigades and regiments and express to them the peculiar anxiety of the Commander of the Forces on the subject.[1]

To the inhabitants he issued a Proclamation in French[1] and Basque on the 1st November, stating that he had given positive orders to prevent the evils which ordinarily accompany invasion by an enemy's army, that they might rest assured that he would carry out the orders given, and he called on them to arrest and bring to Headquarters any soldiers who disobeyed them.[2]

As regards the inhabitants themselves, they were to remain at their homes and take no part in the war.

---

1. See Appendix B.
2. See- Appendix D.

CHAPTER 14

The British Plan of Advance

INSTRUCTIONS ISSUED RELATIVE TO
THE ADVANCE OF THE ALLIED ARMY
ON 10TH NOVEMBER, 1813

The Q.M.G.
To Lieut.-General Sir J. Hope

Vera, 25th Oct., 1813

Previously to the above movements taking place, some additional brigades of artillery[1] will be ordered forward, and placed at your disposal. The 14th Light Dragoons will also be brought up, and probably Major-General Bock's brigade of cavalry will move from Lecumberri a little nearer to the front.

The pontoon train at Irun should likewise be put in a state to move along with the troops under your command, in case circumstances should require it to be used for the passage of the Nivelle. I beg you will ascertain when it can be prepared to move, and give any orders regarding its preparation that may be necessary.

G. *Murray*
Q.M.G.

---

1. A brigade of guns is synonymous with a "battery" of to-day.

To Lieut.-General Sir Rowland Hill

Vera, 17th Oct., 1813

I enclose extract of an instruction which is to be acted upon after the surrender of Pamplona, and when the troops of the right of the army have reached their destinations as pointed out in the instructions I sent you on the 25th instant.

Major-General Colville has been instructed, when the 6th Division moves forward, to send the tents, baggage and other encumbrances into the valley behind Urdax. It would be advisable that you should order the baggage and other encumbrances of the troops under your command to move in the same direction, or into some situation where they may be both in security, and out of the way of the operations of the troops, until the turn affairs take in the course of the day shall have enabled you to judge what further instructions it may be proper to give respecting them.

G. Murray
Q.M.G.

Arrangements preparatory to an intended forward movement of the Army

Upon the actual surrender of Pamplona, the following movements are to take place without further orders:

Major-General Mina is immediately to move forward his troops to the neighbourhood of Roncevaux, where the centre of his division is to be, the right at the same time occupying Orbaiceta, and the left (which should consist of two battalions[1]) occupying the valley of Alduides.

Lieut.-General Sir R. Hill will leave one brigade of *British troops* on the heights, and at the advanced posts of the passes of Roncevaux, to continue there till further orders. The remainder of 2nd Division, including Colonel Ashworth's Portuguese brigade, together with General Morillo's Span-

---

1. Mina's battalions had a strength of from 1,000 to 1,200 men.

ish division, will move by Les Alduides to the valley of Maya. Sir R. Hill will arrange this movement with reference to the following considerations, *viz.*:

The period of arrival (or immediate approach) of General Mina's troops to occupy the positions above pointed out for them. To its being desirable that the above movements should be as much as possible concealed from the enemy; and lastly, to its being intended that the second march of the troops should bring them to the neighbourhood of the pass of Maya, to co-operate, on the following day, with the other troops that are to advance from that quarter.

Two battalions of General Morillo's division should, however, be halted in the neighbourhood of Errazu, to observe the passes in that quarter,[1] and the whole of Lieut.-General Hamilton's Portuguese division will close up to the pass of Maya, when these two battalions have arrived.

The brigade of Portuguese artillery will move by Les Alduides and Maya to act with the above troops.

The brigade of British artillery of the 2nd Division will move back to Pamplona, as will also the detachment of the pontoon train at Espinal.

Colonel Grant's brigade of cavalry is to move up into the valley of Baztan, immediately as each regiment becomes apprised of the surrender of Pamplona. The 4th Regiment of Portuguese cavalry, under Colonel Campbell, will also move into the Baztan valley at the same time by the most convenient route. This regiment will keep up a communication with Pamplona by letter parties.

Major-General Victor Alten's cavalry brigade (immediately on the surrender of Pamplona) will move forward to the valley of the Bidassoa; one regiment occupying Sante-Esterban and Sumbilla, the other regiment Yanci and Lesaca.

---

1. By a letter of 5th November from the Q.M.G. it was left to Hill's discretion to fix as to "what was necessary to place in the posts that cover the Maya and the Baztan valley against Baigorry," and that if Mina could do it the whole of Morillo's division was to move to the Puerto de Maya.

Major-General Alten will keep up a communication by letter parties with the cavalry which will succeed his brigade in the cantonments which it now occupies.

Immediately on the surrender of Pamplona, Lord Edward Somerset will move the Hussar brigade from its present quarters, and will canton it in those now occupied by Major-General Alten's brigade; and in such other adjacent places as it may be necessary to occupy.

Arrangements for the Forward Movement of the Army

The main object of the proposed movement is to place the centre of the army, in the first instance, upon the heights which lie between the villages of Sare and Ascain: and those which form the left bank of the Nivelle river in the neighbourhood of the village of St. Pée. The left of the army, composed of the Spanish corps under Lieut.-General Freyre, and of the troops under the command of Lieut.-General Sir J. Hope, will co-operate with a view to favour this operation of the centre in the manner hereinafter pointed out, as will also the divisions now in the Valley of Maya, and the other troops forming the right of the army under Lieut.-General Sir R. Hill.

Attack on the Centre

The Light Division will assemble before daybreak near the ground now occupied by its outposts, below and to the left of the chapel of La Rhune. From that situation the approach is the easiest to the right flank of the enemy's posts on the rocky ridge called La Petite Rhune.

The division will attack in that direction immediately as the day breaks; and having carried the enemy's position it will establish itself firmly on the Petite Rhune in the most advantageous manner for maintaining that position against any attempt the enemy may make to regain it.

Three mountain guns will be attached to the Light Division for this operation. The division will continue to hold its position on the Petite Rhune until General Alten perceives that the other divisions on the right, which are to move through the village of Sare, have made sufficient progress to be prepared to attack the heathy hills beyond that village; and he will then put his troops in motion to co-operate in the attack of those hills. Brig.-General Longa's troops will move before daybreak to such situations as may have been previously ascertained to be best adapted for bringing them into immediate co-operation with the Light Division when the attack commences.

Major-General Alten will have the superintendence of both divisions.

It will be necessary that a part of General Longa's troops should be pushed down to the left, upon that branch of the mountain which points towards St. Jean de Luz. These troops will oppose the ascent of any force which the enemy may send up the mountain from Ascain, and they will put themselves in communication with the right column of Lieut.-General Freyre's corps which will be ordered to move along the foot of the mountain towards Ascain.

The outposts of the Light Division at the foot of the pass of Vera and those of General Longa's troops, are to remain at their stations until otherwise instructed. The baggage and tents of these two divisions are to remain in their present encampments until further orders.

Major-General Giron will put the troops under his orders in motion exactly at daybreak. The battalions which are at present stationed on the right branch of the Rhune will descend by the ravines in their front towards Sare, and will possess themselves of the lower slopes of the mountain in that direction; as well as of the woods, the gardens and houses on those slopes. They will take care, however, not to descend too much into the village, but will keep in such situations as to be always above the enemy, and they will have strong reserves placed to support their skirmishers.

The main body of General Giron's troops will move forward by the ravine which is on the left of their present encampment.[1] The advance of the column will be favoured on the left flank by the troops which have moved down from the mountain in the manner already mentioned; and General Giron will also throw out such bodies of skirmishers on the flanks of the column as he may find necessary.

As soon as General Giron has made sufficient progress to enable him to do so, he will send three battalions up the ravine which separates the Rhune mountain from the Petite Rhune, now occupied by the enemy. These battalions will ascend the slope of that ridge, where there is a rocky projection about half-way up the bank; and from thence they will gain the top of the ridge in the middle part of it between the two rocky extremities. These battalions will put themselves in communication with the Light Division, and will co-operate with it in driving the enemy down the back part of the rocky ridge.

The remainder of General Giron's troops will continue to move forward by the lower slopes of the Petite Rhune, and by that part of the village of Sare which is situated between the church and the Rhune. In proportion as the column gains ground General Giron will throw his left up the valley which separates the Petite Rhune from the heights which lie behind Sare,[2] between that village and Ascain. This operation will serve to turn the enemy's troops if they remain on the Petite Rhune, and when they are driven from it, it will put General Giron again in connection with the three battalions detached to act against the centre face of the Petite Rhune.

While the left of General Giron's corps is extending up the valley behind the Petite Rhune, the centre and right will advance against the heathy heights beyond Sare. General Giron's column will be accompanied by three mountain guns.

The 4th Division will be at daybreak on the present encamping ground of General Giron's troops. It will move for-

1. This was on the southern part of the Monho ridge, S.W. of Ste. Barbe.
2. i.e. that leading to the Col St. Ignace.

ward from thence to the attack of the enemy's right redoubt (Ste. Barbe) which covers the village of Sare. After carrying that redoubt, the division will advance through the village in the direction of the church. It will then continue its progress so as to leave on its left the enemy's camp of huts on the brown bank behind Sare; and advancing against the hills beyond the village, it will ascend them so that its left may co-operate with General Giron's right in the attack on the large heathy height (Signal redoubt hill), whilst the right and centre of the division ascend a little more to the right, where the enemy's position recedes, and where the slopes begin to be enclosed and wooded to the top (i.e. on both sides of the Col de Mendionde).

The 4th Division will be accompanied by a brigade or troop of artillery, to be employed in the first instance against the enemy's right redoubt. The baggage and tents of the 4th Division, and of General Giron's corps, are to be left in the present encampments of the divisions until further orders.

The 7th Division will descend from the Puerto de Echalar, and will afterwards move along by the ravine which is upon the right of the tongue of land on which General Giron's troops are now encamped. The division must be in this ravine before daybreak. It will attack the enemy's left redoubt (Granada) which covers Sare. Having carried it, the division will direct its march so as to keep at some distance to the right flank of the 4th, and, passing by the lower end of the village of Sare, will ascend the hills beyond it by that part of the enemy's position which projects towards us and where the ground is a good deal intersected by woods and enclosures, and where the slope appears to be longer and more gradual than in the other parts of the range of heights.

The 7th Division will be accompanied by a brigade or troop of artillery, to be employed in the first instance against the enemy's left redoubt. The baggage and tents of the division will not descend from the Puerto de Echalar until orders to that effect are given.

The 3rd Division will move forward by the road which leads on the left bank of the Nivelle from Urdax and Zugaramurdi towards St. Pée.

It will be the business of this division to co-operate with the 7th by covering its right flank, and by otherwise aiding its progress as may be necessary. As the attack advances, the 3rd Division will push forward some troops into the ravine by which the Nivelle passes through the hills, and breaks the connection between the heights beyond Sare and the long ridge which the enemy occupies behind Ainhoa. There is a bridge across the Nivelle where it passes through the hills, which the 3rd Division will endeavour to get possession of, so as to prevent the enemy using that communication between the camps behind Sare and those behind Ainhoa, and for the further purpose of securing its use for our own troops in their subsequent operations.

It is probable that the artillery with the 7th Division may be most advantageously used against the enemy's left redoubt, from situations between the lines of march of the 7th and 3rd Divisions; in which case it will be the business of both divisions to attend to the protection of the guns.

The 3rd Division should be formed behind its own outposts before daylight, so as to move forward when the day breaks. It will keep up communication at all times with the 6th Division which will be on its right on the other side of the Nivelle.

As the advance of General Giron's corps on the one hand, and that of the 3rd Division upon the other, will turn both flanks of the two redoubts in front of Sare, it may be expected that the progress of these divisions will shake the confidence of the troops holding these works, and facilitate very considerably the attacks which the 4th and 7th Divisions are ordered to make on them. The tents of the 3rd Division may be moved down to Zugaramurdi; but all other encumbrances are to be left in the present encampment of the division until further orders.

When the heights beyond Sare have been gained, the corps employed against them, *viz*.:

The Light Division and General Longa's troops
General Giron's corps
The 4th Division,
The 7th Division
The 3rd Division

will establish themselves firmly on these heights, pushing forward at first detachments only in pursuit of the enemy; and in that situation of things these troops will receive fresh instructions as to their further movements.

Major-General V. Alten's cavalry brigade will act with this part of the army; and a squadron of Colonel Grant's brigade will be attached to the 3rd Division in its first movements.

CO-OPERATION OF THE TROOPS FROM THE
VALLEY OF MAYA, AND OF OTHERS ATTACHED
FOR THE PRESENT TO THE RIGHT OF THE ARMY

The 6th Division will move from its positions in the night, so as to be prepared to advance from the neighbourhood of the present outposts of the Portuguese brigade of the division at daybreak. The division will move against the right of the enemy's position behind Ainhoa, and will keep up communication from its left flank with the 3rd Division.

Lieut.-General Hamilton's Portuguese division, and the other troops on the right of the army under Lieut.-General Sir R. Hill, will co-operate with the 6th Division. Sir R. Hill will accordingly order these troops to move in the night from the pass of Maya into the situations most favourable for their further advance.

The attack in this quarter is to be made in echelon from the left; the 6th Division leading, and directing itself against the right of the enemy's position behind Ainhoa. The other troops will support the 6th Division; refusing the right, but at the same time threatening the enemy in that direction, so as to make him apprehend an attack, and prevent him throwing his whole force to his right flank.

Colonel Grant's cavalry brigade, less one squadron, will act with the troops employed against the enemy's position on the right bank of the Nivelle.

When the troops under Sir R. Hill have made themselves masters of the enemy's position behind Ainhoa, they will establish themselves there, and wait for further instructions. Sir R. Hill will in the meantime secure his right by occupying the large square redoubt near the centre of the enemy's position, and will send a part of the cavalry to ascertain the direction of the enemy's retreat and push patrols, if possible, to Souraide and Espelette.

It is intended that that part of General Morillo's corps which moves up to the pass of Maya should act upon the hills, beyond where the outposts of the 6th Division now extend. This will alarm the enemy for the left of position: and should he actually withdraw his troops from the hills, the object of Morillo's attack, the occupation of these by him will assist the operations of the other troops under Sir R. Hill's command. The baggage and tents of 6th Division are to be moved into the valley behind Urdax when the troops advance, and Sir R. Hill will order the baggage and tents of the other troops under his command into such situations, in the same direction, as will place them in security, and out of the way of the troops, until he thinks it proper to send further orders.

CO-OPERATION OF THE TROOPS FORMING
THE LEFT OF THE ARMY

One division of Lieut.-General Freyre's corps will move towards Ascain; it will assemble before daylight behind the small detached hill called Arrequico Borda,[1] upon which hill

---

1. The basque word *Borda* signifies a house or isolated farm.

there is now an advanced post of Longa's troops. From thence it will advance at daybreak, keeping close to the lower slopes of that spur from the Rhune mountain which stretches towards Ascain. The road it will take passes a small house called Paragein Borda, and proceeds thence to Ascain. It will detach some troops up the slopes of the mountain on its right, in the direction of a house called Mendionda Borda, and will endeavour to get in connection with General Longa's troops in that part of the mountain.

The remainder of General Freyre's corps will assemble in front of the height called Arrequico Borda, and will advance from thence at daybreak by a road which lies a little to our left of the house of Jolimont, and which leads towards a farm called Choucouten Borda. This column will be accompanied by artillery to act against that which the enemy may have in his works.

Lieut.-General Freyre will bear in mind, however, that it is not intended to push this column forward so as to force the enemy's works if they appear to be prepared to make a good defence; for this part of General Freyre's corps is meant less as a column of attack, than as a reserve in retired echelon to the right division ordered to march towards Ascain. Its situation near Jolimont will enable it to give support to the right column, with which it will communicate by pushing strong detachments into the ravine that separates them, and in the direction of a house surrounded by many poplars. At the same time, however, by threatening an attack on the works in the direction of Choucouten Borda, the left column will hinder the enemy from detaching troops from there to any other point. General Freyre will keep one battalion in reserve near the house called Escola, which is surrounded by the ditch of an old French redoubt, and where there is at present a Spanish piquet. A battalion should also be stationed in reserve on the heights called Arrequico.

The troops under Lieut.-General Sir J. Hope will act in three columns as follows:

The centre column will attack the heights which lie to our left of the village of Urrugne; and having gained them, a part of the troops are to be pushed forward a little, so as to occupy the most advantageous points on the left bank of the rivulet which runs between the heights of Urrugne and those of Ciboure, and enters the sea near Socoa. The troops of this column when halted will front towards Ciboure and St. Jean de Luz; and Sir J. Hope will see that they are so placed that they are not exposed to artillery fire from the works which cover Ciboure and the convent of Bordagain.

The left column will act between the heights of Urrugne and the sea coast. When halted it will face towards Socoa.

The right column will move so as to keep up communication with the troops under General Freyre, and it will, at the same time, threaten the front of the enemy's encampment on the right bank of the rivulet of Urrugne, and to our right of the great road which leads from that village to St. Jean de Luz.

Sir J. Hope will bear in mind, however, that it is not intended that operations in this quarter should be pushed to a real attack, and that it is meant only to fix the attention of the enemy, and prevent his detaching troops to support other points of his line.

Should it happen, however, that the success of the other attacks on the enemy induce him to abandon any of the positions or works he holds on the left bank of the Nivelle, between Ascain and Socoa, General Freyre and General Sir J. Hope will consider themselves authorized to occupy the ground which the enemy abandons; and they will, in that case, advance the troops towards the line of the Nivelle, so far as this can be effected with advantage, and without committing the troops in an attack against any point strongly held, or immediately under the protection of the enemy's works.

The baggage and tents of the left of the army are to remain in the present encampments until Sir J. Hope and General Freyre give further orders. Sir J. Hope will place an officer's detachment of cavalry in the neighbourhood of Jolimont, near the bottom of the hill by which the road goes through Brigadier Longa's present encampment to Vera. This detachment is intended to keep up the communication with the centre of the army, in the first instance through Vera, and afterwards by Ascain, should that communication become open.

G. *Murray,* Q.M.G.

The following MEMO OF ORDERS TO BE SENT FOR MOVEMENT ON 8TH NOVEMBER UPON SARE, *4th November, 1813, was written by Wellington and contains some points not dealt with in the undated arrangement.*

Supposing Sir R. Hill to put his troops in motion on the 6th, attack should take place on the 8th.

Colonel Grant to be apprised that Sir R. Hill is directed to order the 13th Light Dragoons into the valley of Baztan; and to be instructed to close up his brigade upon the 6th Division towards Maya, that it may be at hand to act with the troops under Sir R. Hill on the morning of the 8th. The artillery under Lieut.-Colonel Tulloh to be ordered to move forward, so as to be on the top of the pass of Maya (but concealed from the enemy) on 7th instant, that it may be prepared to act on 8th. The three mountain guns at Elizondo to be ordered to move likewise to the pass of Maya, that they may accompany the 6th Division when it descends from thence to the station whence it is to move forward at daybreak on 8th.

Orders to be sent through Sir S. Cotton for the 4th Portuguese Cavalry to move forward so as to arrive in the Baztan valley on 7th instant or morning of 8th.

Major-General V. Alten to be instructed to move the 18th Hussars into the valley of the Bidassoa on 6th instant, and to canton the brigade in Yanci, Echalar, and Lesaca. Lord E. Somerset to be directed to occupy the quarters quitted by the 18th Hussars, together with such other cantonment as may place the brigade most *à portée* to pass into the Bidassoa valley should it be so ordered. One squadron of the brigade is to be established at Santesteban on 7th, from which letter parties are to be sent to Vera and Echalar, and also to an intermediate point between these places and Santesteban. These letter parties to be in their places as early as possible on morning of 8th. Major Gardiner's troop of artillery to canton in neighbourhood of Lecumberri.

Sir J. Hope to be instructed to order forward Captain Greene's and Captain Cairne's brigade of artillery in sufficient time to enable them to act with the troops under his orders on morning of 8th, and also to direct Major-General Vandeleur to order up the 16th Light Dragoons in sufficient time for the same object. Orders to be given for the movement of Major-General Bradford's brigade to the vicinity of Vera on 7th instant, that it may take the situation allotted to it at daybreak the following morning.

The reserve of small arms ammunition on mules to move forward so as to be at Vera on morning of 8th. Three mountain guns to join the Light Division on 7th, three also to join General Giron's troops on 7th. The three brigades of artillery at Vera to move forward on 7th instant to the most convenient station on the newly repaired road in front of 4th Division.

The several divisions to be apprised of the date when they are to move. The detachment of the Royal Staff Corps with the left to be placed at Sir J. Hope's disposal; the detachment at Enderlazza to move to Sare, and act with the centre of the army.

Wellington

MEMORANDUM

Vera, 6th November, 1813

The forward movement of the army (the instructions for which have been already circulated) is to take place on morning of —— The general officers to whom these instructions have been communicated will make their arrangements accordingly.

The clearness of the nights will facilitate the movements of the troops to their assembly positions. If, however, the morning of the —— should prove foggy, the operations are not to commence at daybreak as directed, but the signal for their commencement on the right of the army and in the centre, is to be the opening of the artillery with the 4th Division against the enemy's redoubts in front of Sare.

In case there should be no fog on the Rhune, General Alten is, notwithstanding, to delay the attack if there is a fog in the valleys below, until the 4th Division artillery has opened as before mentioned. He will be careful, therefore, so to place his troops that they may be concealed from the enemy until the above signal is heard.[2]

General Freyre will commence his operations at the same time as those of the Light Division; and as General Freyre may not hear the firing of the artillery in front of Sare, General Alten will take measures to inform him as speedily as possible of the commencement of the attack.

Upon Sir R. Hill's arrival in the Valley of Maya he will assume command of the troops destined to act against the enemy's position behind Ainhoa; and Marshal Beresford will take the immediate direction, on the morning of the attack of the 3rd, 7th, and 4th Divisions.

G. Murray, Q.M.G.

---

1. Certain officers were detailed as an observing party on the summit of the Grande Rhune, and very detailed instructions given them as to what they were to observe and report. The Light Division was to find a party of messengers to carry the reports down the mountain, and the 4th Division a party to carry them to the camp of Giron's corps, where a party of the Staff Corps was stationed to carry the reports to Wellington.

CHAPTER 15

The Battle of the Nivelle

Sunrise (lat. 43° N.) 6.50 a.m. local mean time.
Sunset 4.40 p.m.
Full moon 8th November.

The following night (9/10 November) which a brilliant full moon rendered as bright as day.
—Woolwright, History of 57th Regiment.

It was a most beautiful moonlight morning; and so clear that it was difficult to say at what moment night ended and daylight began.
—Batty.

The day broke with great splendour.
—Napier.

The day was beautiful.
—Larpent.

The wind was a steady fresh breeze towards the sea, that is towards our left. (i.e. an easterly wind.)
—Frazer's letter of 11th Nov.

Larpent's Journal
Vera, 9th Nov., 1813

Your English mail is nothing thought of . . . . We have to-day much greater news from the French side, which is believed by everyone here, and by the

French army we are told (by deserters) namely that Bonaparte is beaten back to the Rhine with the loss of three divisions.

10th Nov

I dined with Lord Wellington last night. He was all gaiety and spirits, and only said on leaving the room, 'Remember! At four in the morning.'

The news of Napoleon's defeat at Leipzig had reached Bayonne and the French army about 8th or 9th November. Between 3 and 4 a.m. on the 10th the divisions of the allied army, aided by the light of a nearly full moon and a cloudless sky, were silently moving to their respective assembly points on a front of about twelve miles.[1]

THE DEMONSTRATION OF
THE ALLIED LEFT WING

Sir John Hope's corps consisted of the 1st Division, Howard; the 5th Division, Hay; Aylmer's brigade; Wilson's Portuguese brigade; Vandeleur's Cavalry brigade; a regiment of Bock's German Legion Cavalry and several Horse and Field batteries.

Before daybreak the troops of the left wing had moved up to their outpost line, where they lay down awaiting the signal to attack. Shortly before sunrise a battery of horse artillery opened fire against the French works which had been thrown up around the ruined chapel of Socorry. Immediately the whole line of the allied outposts advanced and commenced a sharp attack on those of the enemy being followed by the columns. The 5th Division on the extreme left along the coast, with the 2nd Guards brigade on their right. Halket's brigade of the German Legion and Aylmer's

---

1. Diary of a commissariat officer. "This grand movement was made with a quietness and secrecy almost incredible. The tents were left standing and fires burning."

brigade prolonged the line to the main road. South of this were Hinuber's Legion brigade, the 1st Guards brigade, with Wilson's brigade on the extreme right.

When the British artillery had nearly silenced that of the French in the Socorry redoubt, which was also held by two battalions, Halket moved round the hill to the allied left of the redoubt menacing its rear, whilst the strong Guards' piquet, which had always been maintained facing the redoubt, advanced against its front. The French kept up a hot musketry fire from the works and abattis, but the British troops rushing forward seized the post and drove the French down the hill to the edge of the Bordagain position.

Whilst this was going on the 85th of Aylmer's brigade attacked and carried the village of Urrugne. Being ordered to hold it at all hazards, the regiment tore down the barricade of casks filled with stones and earth across the entrance to the village from which they had driven its defenders, trundled them down to the northern end of the village and there barricaded that entrance.[1] As soon asthe French had evacuated Socorry the 5th Division advanced along the northern spur which springs from the Croix-des-Bouquets heights, carried an entrenchment and abattis placed across the spur, drove the garrison back to Socoa, and pushed forward towards the inundation which covered the Ciboure defences, against which a brisk fire of infantry and artillery was kept up by Sir John Hope's orders.[2]

Meanwhile the right column acting to the south of the main road under Major-General Howard had been split up in several small columns and was advancing against the entrenchments on the ridge which extends southwards from Urtubie towards Olhette and Ascain. The engagement here was entirely one of skirmishers and artillery; the line of allied light infantry several times crossed the Unxain valley,

---

1. Gleig, *The Subaltern.*
2. Batty. "By the spirit with which it was answered it was evident the French apprehended that the onset would be followed by an assault."

falling back before the French counterattacks and again advancing. This went on most of the day all along the allied line. Gleig thus describes it:

It would be hard to conceive a more animating military spectacle than met the eye that day, as it turned to right and left tracing the British line. On this occasion our line of skirmishers extended about a mile in both directions, all spread out in irregular order, and firing independently as a good target presented itself. On the side of the French all was apparent confusion. Yet the French *tirailleurs* are by no means in disorder when they appear so. They are admirable skirmishers, and gave our people this day a good deal of employment before they again betook themselves to the heights.[1] It was evident from the numerous solid bodies of troops which kept their ground along the enemy's front that no force had been sent from the right of Soult's army to the assistance of his left. . . . At length Soult appeared to have discovered he had little to dread upon his right, for about 3 p.m. we could observe a heavy column begin its march to the left; at the same time, as if to cover the movement, the enemy's skirmishers advanced. Again we drove them in.

This column, whose movement was seen, was the French and German brigades of Villatte's division, with Soult and some reserve artillery commencing their march towards Serres. The skirmishing along the line continued till about an hour after sunset, when the allied troops retired to their previous positions. During the afternoon the Sloops *Challenger, Vesuvius, Sparrow* and *Racer* appeared off Socoa and opened fire on the fort, but the swell was too great to permit them to come into close range and they withdrew.

---

1. Gleig. *The Subaltern.*

On the right of Hope's corps that of Freyre had advanced in two columns. That on the right of one division, moving from below the Mandale mountain, had as its objective the heights on the left bank of the Nivelle which command the village of Ascain and the bridge there. The left column, moving from the Calvaire hill, was comprised of the remainder of the corps. It was to use the road which passes to the west of Jolimont, and leads towards Choucouten Farm and St. Jean de Luz. Its advance thus pointed towards the left flank of Reille's corps; but, by Wellington's order, its commander was warned not to attack if the enemy seemed prepared to make a good defence, and he was to consider his force as a reserve to the right column.

Between 8 and 9 a.m. the right column was advancing towards Ascain. Being opposed by the Spanish brigade of Villatte's division it drove this brigade back towards Ascain. To its assistance Darricau sent the Italian brigade, and by its aid the Spaniards were able to cross the Nivelle by the bridge of boats near Dorria, when both brigades retired to Serres. Freyre's and Longa's divisions then took position on the heights from which, and the village of Ascain, they kept up a fire on the bridge and the nearest Serres defences, "which was not without moral effect,"[1] as until evening Darricau with his division and the two foreign brigades, in all about 10,000 men, was held in check and immobilized by some 6,000 Spaniards on the left bank of the river.

Freyre's left column does not appear to have advanced much farther than the high ground above Jolimont and Olhette. Its position there commanded the road leading from the French line, blocking any advance from it and also covering the line of retreat of the right column. Its artillery throughout the day kept up fire on a French battery placed

---

1. *Vidal de la Blache,* Vol. I.

to cover the approach from the south.[1] Both it and the right column fully fulfilled their purposes.

The French retired from Ascain in the afternoon of 10th and it was occupied by Longa's division. As this division pillaged the village during the night Wellington sent the division back into Spain beyond the Ebro.

Capture of the Petite Rhune by the Light Division

As the French retained possession of the Petite Rhune, they held a fortified position almost in the centre of the allied line, and in advance of that taken up by their army, it was manifestly necessary that this position must be captured before the general attack on the enemy's main positions was delivered, because it barred the approach to the Col St. Ignace, by which alone the Light Division could make a frontal attack as outlined in Wellington's orders.

This was the task allotted to the Light Division. Longa's Spanish division, which was also under the command of General Alten, had as its objective, in conjunction with Freyre's right column, the high ground above the village of Ascain. In position there it could oppose any troops sent from Serres to reinforce the Petite Rhune garrison, or act against the Light Division.

The Petite Rhune was held by the 4th Light (two battalions), 40th and 34th regiments of Barbot's brigade of Maransin's division. The 4th held the Mouiz redoubt, the trenches about it, and part of the traverse which connected the Mouiz

---

1. Batty. "Nearly opposite the point to which the extreme right of the left wing extended, the French had a remarkably strong redoubt to cover the approach to their position by the Vera road; a brigade of artillery on a hill opposite kept up a hot fire of shot and shells against this redoubt for the greater part of the day, but it was tenaciously held by the enemy, although we could see they were suffering greatly from the fire of the artillery."

with the works on the Petite Rhune itself, and had two companies in reserve behind the redoubt. The 40th held the Petite Rhune defences, part of the traverse with a reserve behind it, and the rocky post in the col between the two Rhunes which commands the mule track which ascends from Sare to the Mouiz. The 34th had various companies spread along the spur by which this track ascends. The 50th, the remaining regiment of the brigade, was in the camp of the division about the Col de Sare.

In the dusk of the evening of 9th November the units of the Light Division concentrated from their several camps, and moved across the lower slopes of the Grande Rhune until within about 2 miles from the Petite. Here they halted, put out piquets and the men lay down to sleep. A full hour before daybreak they moved forward silently, and, forming a line of quarter columns, lay down behind the last lateral spur of the Great Rhune within half-musket shot of the French piquets on the other side of a deep ravine. The 3rd/95th Rifles and three mountain guns had been previously sent to the summit of the Grande Rhune; during the night two of these guns were brought about half-way down the northern slope of the mountains.

Alten's orders for the attack were that the 1st Brigade under Major-General Kempt was to drive the French from the Petite Rhune, whilst the 2nd under Colonel Colborne was to turn the Mouiz plateau by the left.

> The sky was almost cloudlessly clear, the twilight rapidly brightening and the outline of the mountains had become distinctly marked, when the flash and echoing report of a mountain 3-pounder on the extreme point of the Rhune gave the signal to advance.[1]

Springing from their concealment, the Rifle battalions and Cacadores rushed down the slope into the saddle between

---

1. Moorsom, *History of 52nd Regiment*.

the Rhunes,[1] followed by the rest of the division in battalion columns.[2] On the right were the 43rd and 17th Portuguese. Having descended, Major William Napier, commanding the 43rd, sent two companies across the marsh at the foot of the slope to assist in keeping down the fire from the lower works on the west slope of the Petite Rhune, whilst the rest of the regiment turned it by the right at the double. Having done so, Napier ordered a short halt to let the men get their breath, and then assailed the works and carried them one by one until that on the highest point, called the Donjon, which was separated from the lower by a deep cleft in the rock, was reached, and here again the men were given a halt. Meanwhile the 17th Portuguese, originally detailed as a support to the 43rd, seeing the rapid progress made by the latter, pushed up the valley towards the rocky post held by the French at the eastern end of the saddle. Observing this advance the 3rd/95th Rifles on the Great Rhune rushed down the slope covered by the fire of the mountain guns, and with the 17th drove the French from the post.

On the left were the 52nd and 2nd/95th. The 52nd

hastened straight down the slope in its front, but as soon as it had crossed the rocky water-course at the bottom, brought up its right shoulders, and pushed rapidly on, in a line nearly parallel to the water-course on its left and to the French works about 500 yards off" in its right. The enemy, either in the darkness of the mountain shadows did not see, or perceiving, had not the presence of mind to attempt to check this bold flank movement. The 52nd gained the line of the extreme flank of the French works, brought up its left shoulders, scrambled up the rocky slope, and stood in rear of the enemy's right on the plateau of the Petite Rhune."[3]

1. Maransin's Report, November 1813.
2. Leach, J., *Rough Sketches.*
3. Moorsom, *History of 52nd Regiment.*

During this movement of the 52nd, the trenches and out-works on the Mouiz plateau and the Traverse were engaged by the 2nd/95th and the Cacadores which kept up the communication between the 52nd and the 43rd. On reaching the plateau the 52nd was attacked by the reserve companies of the 4th Light, but they could only contain the enemy for a few minutes. Meanwhile the Donjon was taken by the 43rd, and General Barbot gave the order to evacuate the position and retreat to the divisional camp near the Col de Sare,[1] and soon "the French defenders of the last of their Pyrenean summits were rushing into the huge rough punch-bowl which is bounded by the eastern and western spurs of the Petite Rhune, followed by the 1st/95th Rifles into the valley below."[2]

The fight had been short but sharp. "The whole place was carried within the time required to walk over it; and in less than half an hour from the commencement of the attack it was in our possession."[3] It was a whole division against four battalions, but the allied loss in officers was severe, as eleven fell against sixty-seven other ranks. Eyewitnesses deposed to the gallantry of the French officers and their efforts to make their men stand. By 8 a.m. the Petite Rhune was in possession of the Light Division.

After the evacuation of the works by the French, the Light Division concentrated on the Mouiz plateau, and remained there until the divisions of the centre had "made sufficient progress to be prepared to attack the enemy's main position." The division then moved down towards the Col St. Ignace to attack the right flank of Taupin's division above the col. Napier states the time as 9.30 a.m. Kincaid says, "about mid-day the division advanced to the grand attack,"[4] which would appear to be more correct.

---

1. Maransin's Report, November 1813. *"L'Etoil (redoubt) engagee ne pouvant plus tenir, est evacuee par ordre du General Barbot, qui effectue sa retraite sur le camp de la 2ᵉ brigade."*
2. Moorsom.
3. Kincaid, *Adventures in the Rifle Brigade.*
4. Kincaid, *Adventures in the Rifle Brigade.*

CHAPTER 16

The Attack of the Centre Corps

Clausel's Corps	4th Division	Rey's brigade	12th Light,$_2$ 32nd,$_2$ 43rd,$_2$
	Conroux	Baurot's brigade	45th, 55th, 58th
	5th Division	Barbot's brigade	4th Light, 34th, 40th,$_2$ 50th
	Maransin	Rouget's brigade	27th, 59th, 130th,$_2$
	6th Division	Dature's brigade	9th Light,$_2$ 26th, 47th,$_2$
	Taupin	Dein's brigade	31st Light,$_2$ 70th, 88th

At daybreak on 10th November Clausel's corps was distributed as follows: Three battalions of Barbot's brigade, the 4th Light and the two battalions of 40th held, as we have seen, the Petite Rhune. The 34th was distributed by companies along the spur which falls from near the Petite Rhune towards Sare, and on which is a mule track from Sare to the Mouiz plateau. Rouget's brigade, with the exception of the 130th, was at its camp at the col de Sare to the French right of the then road from Sare to Ascain, and with it was the 50th of Barbot's brigade. The 130th was in a hutted camp on an underfeature to the north of Sare, called in Wellington's orders "the brown bank."[1]

Rey's brigade of Conroux's division found the garrisons of the Ste. Barbe and Granada redoubts, two companies and two guns in each, whilst the rest of the brigade held the entrenchments covering the village of Sare, the right of their

---

1. Maransin's Report, November 1813. *"Les 50me, 27me et 59me de ligne était au camp situé au Col de Sare, à la droite du chemin d'Ascain; enfin, le 130me au camp en arriere de Sare."*

outposts being in touch with the companies of the 34th holding the lower part of the Rhune spur. Baurot's brigade occupied the left of Clausel's section from the Louis XIV redoubt to the Nivelle River. Taupin's division was on the right of the main position; thus at the opening of the engagement this division and Baurot's brigade of Conroux's were the only infantry on it.

Before entering into any details of the fighting it would seem advisable here to notice what appears to be an error made by some writers who describe the battle, and regard the Col de Sare as identical with the Col St. Ignace, stating that it was to the latter col that Barbot's troops retreated when driven from the Petite Rhune by the Light Division. Thus Captain Vidal de la Blache states that they retreated by the spur leading to the Col St. Ignace,[1] and Sir John Fortescue in his history of the British army makes the retreat to be to the same col.

Now the mass of Rouget's brigade was not at St. Ignace, but at the camp of Sare, as is definitely stated in Maransin's report. This camp he locates as being to the French right of the then road from Sare to Ascain. A reference to a map will show that from the Larraldea hill—the "petit mamelon" of Maransin's report—an underfeature runs northwards and then bends due east ending in "the brown bank." At the bend there is a depression, and over this passed the then road to Ascain, which was at a considerably lower level than the present road. On this underfeature was the camp of Sare in two parts, one to the south of the col and the other on "the brown bank" to the north and east of it.

To place the camp of Sare about the Col de St. Ignace is to make that part of Maransin's report dealing with the fighting about Sare almost incomprehensible.

Shortly after daybreak the three batteries which had come

---

1. *L'evacuation de L'Espagne et l'invasion dans le Midi*, Vol. I. *"La masse confuse en retraite qui refluait vers le gros de la division Maransin, le long du contrefort qui mene au Col Saint-Ignace."*

from Vera under the command of Lieut.-Colonel Frazer, Ross's troop of Royal Horse Artillery, Sympher's and Douglas's field batteries, covered by an advanced party from the 4th Division, opened fire on the Ste. Barbe redoubt.

The French having hastily withdrawn their piquets,. Ross's troop was able to move on to the ridge at the northern extremity of which the redoubt stands, and open fire within 400 yards of it. It was not however till after an hour's firing, that the enemy, seeing our column approaching, abandoned it.[1]

The guns then changed position, and opened on the Granada redoubt, which its garrison "abandoned with discreditable precipitation" after being under fire for a quarter of an hour. It was now about 7.45 a.m. Though the ground was difficult the infantry divisions were advancing with great celerity,"[2] Giron's Spaniards on the left across the lower slopes of the Rhune, with their right flank covered by the 4th Division led by Anson's brigade, whose direction point was the church of Sare. On its right was the 7th Division, which was to pass to the east of the village, and further eastwards, the 3rd Division from Zugaramurdi; connection between the 3rd and 7th Divisions being kept by the 94th Regiment under Lieut.-Colonel Lloyd.

As ordered, each division had to form its own reserve; a measure almost obligatory owing to the special nature of the ground, and the then limited range of firearms and guns. As was customary, divisions were preceded by an advanced line of skirmishers composed of the light companies of each brigade, the attached rifle companies (5/60th Rifles) and the Portuguese cacadores.

The redoubts in front of Sare having been captured, the 4th Division, supported by the fire of the British guns on the

---

1. *Letters of Sir A. Frazer during the Peninsula and Waterloo Campaigns,* 11th November, 1813, 11 a.m.
2. Frazer's letter of the 11th November, 1813.

Ste. Barbe hill, advanced against the village and its environs, with Giron's corps on its left and the 7th Division moving to the east of the village on its right. Rey's brigade put up a stout defence, but numbers and the outflanking movement on either side obliged retreat; and Clausel ordered Rey to retire and join Baurot's brigade on the left of the main position; the 4th Division then occupied Sare at about 9 a.m.

Whilst this had been going on, the battalions of Barbot's brigade were in full retreat from the Petite Rhune, towards the camp of Rouget's brigade, and Giron's three battalions as ordered had ascended the spur from the Rhune and gained touch with the Light Division. To assist the 34th in covering the retreat of the Petite Rhune battalions, the 50th on the first shot being fired[1] had moved to the Larraldia hill in support of the 34th companies there. These were soon hotly engaged with Giron's left column, and with the 50th were gradually pushed up the valley leading *to* the Col St. Ignace by the Spaniards, who picked up on the way some of the 1st/95th Rifles who had followed the fugitives down the slope. As they approached the col they came under fire from Taupin's guns on the ridge above, but taking advantage of cover and moving in small parties, were able to ensconce themselves in houses and copses above the col and the deep ravine below it.

When Clausel ordered Rey's brigade to retire and rejoin its division on the extreme left, he also directed Taupin to man the defences allotted to his division. When this was done, the division was distributed as follows. The 70th held the St. Ignace redoubt and that close to it, half the battalion in each; the 9th held the trenches below the redoubts on the slopes facing the Rhune, the 26th those facing towards Sare, the 47th$_2$, the works on the extreme right of the position above Ascain, and the 88th the signal redoubt. Taupin was also ordered to send 100 men to hold the Lou-

---

1. Maransin's Report.

is XIV redoubt, and to keep his reserve, the 31st Light, 2 battalions, ready to move to that redoubt if circumstances rendered it necessary.[1]

Meanwhile, the 3rd Division, whose assembly position in front of Zugaramurdi was about 3 miles from the bridge of Amots over country somewhat easier than that traversed by the divisions on its left, was rapidly advancing with little or no opposition against the extreme left of Clausel's position. Having crossed the Harane stream and the Sare—St. Pée road to the east of the hamlet of Ihalar, where a detachment was sent along the road to seize the bridge of Amots, the division moved round behind the long wooded spur which descends from the heights to the St. Pée road to the east of Sare. It then attacked the Ste. Madeleine redoubt hill and the batteries commanding the road and the bridge with Keane's brigade supported by the rest of the division.

The fight was a stiff one, and Keane's brigade suffered heavily, especially the 87th regiment under Lieut.-Colonel Gough. But Conroux's men, especially such as had been in the fighting about Sare,[2] were shaken, their beloved leader was mortally wounded,[3] and about 10 a.m. the division broke and retired along the Nivelle towards St. Pée, leaving the heights and the bridge in possession of the 3rd Division. At 9.30 a.m. Clausel, seeing the allied columns at Sare and below Istilarte preparing to move against the heights between the Louis XIV redoubt and the bridge of Amots, sent a battery of artillery to the east of the redoubt, and ordered Maransin to immediately send the 59th into the

---

1. Clausel's Report, 11th November, 1813.
2. It seems likely that not a few of Rey's brigade, which had been spread in a long front before Sare, could not or would not rejoin their division. Vidal de la Blache quotes from a report of the Prefet de Pau, "that from 10 a.m. fugitives of Conroux's division were passing through the woods of St. Pée and Ustaritz."
3. Lapene. *"Qui rappelait par sa simplicité les generaux de la Republique."* General Baron N. Conroux de Pepinville died of his wounds the following day, aged 35 years.

redoubt, then held by a party of conscripts, and place Barbot's brigade to the east and Rouget's to the west of it.[1] As the units of Barbot's brigade were collected they proceeded to their position and were followed by Rouget's, the movement being covered by the 130th, which held the brown bank. Taupin was also ordered to be ready to send half of his reserve, the two battalions of the 31st Light, to the redoubt if it appeared to be seriously attacked.

About 9.30 a.m. the 4th and 7th Divisions and Giron's right column commenced their advance against the French main position, Giron and the left column of 4th Division against the brown bank, the remainder of the 4th Division against the Louis XIV redoubt, and the 7th Division against the heights to the allied right of it. The advance came under heavy fire from the enemy's field and heavy guns in the entrenchments, which could not be replied to "as it was some time before we could get the guns up, and we obviously had not the best of it."[2] But the allied light troops pressing on drove the 130th from the hutted camp on the brown hill about 10 a.m., under the shelter of which the column rested for a while,[3] covered by a long line of skirmishers clinging to such cover as they could get behind banks, hedges and trees. The advance was then continued, Giron's right column and the left of the 4th Division against the Col de Mendionde, and the remainder of the 4th and Giron's main body against the Louis XIV redoubt, the capture of which was the task assigned to the 20th Regiment.

Sergeant Cooper, 7th Fusiliers, 4th Division,[4] thus describes the British advance.

---

1. Clausel's Report, 11th November, 1813.
2. *Letters of Sir A. Frazer.*
3. Frazer's letter, 11th November. "The infantry moving up forced a kind of lower ridge in the centre of the position (the brown hill). Here, however, it became necessary to shelter the troops under the steep edge of this ridge, the enemy still playing with vivacity from four field and as many heavy guns in his redoubt."
4. Cooper, *Rough Notes of Seven Campaigns.*

The tide of war was rolling furiously onward, and the advance of our troops from hedge to hedge was really brilliant. If there was a stop for a moment or two, the next thing was a run and a cheer.

The French made a resolute and protracted defence about the redoubt. "Indeed they were very pertinacious," writes Major Mills of the 40th. But Maransin's division was doubtless somewhat shaken, his guns had been silenced by Ross's troop, the only ones which had been able to reach the summit, Barbot's brigade by the experience of the morning, and all by the retreat of Conroux's division. The 7th Division, having gained the heights, came down on his front and on his now-exposed left flank, and drove the division down into the ravine behind, and the Louis XIV redoubt was taken about 11 a.m., after what Clausel says was the third attack; whereupon the division, with the 27th and 130th of Rouget's brigade as rear-guard, retired towards St. Pée. During the fighting about the redoubt General Maransin was taken prisoner, but in the confusion managed to escape. The losses of the division during the day were 132 killed and 703 wounded.

Clausel therefore had now but one division, that of Taupin, left in his fighting line on the heights. He had always expected that Darricau's division from Serres would arrive to his assistance, and hoping that he would be able to rally the two retreating divisions, he considered he could hold what remained of his position, and informed Taupin of his intention.

Having captured the Louis XIV redoubt, the next effort of the Allies was made against the Col de Mendionde, by which the track from Sare to Harosteguia crosses the heights.[1] For this purpose the 4th Division and Giron's Spaniards were massed towards it. Seeing this, Clausel placed the two battalions of the 31st Light across the col, and ordered Taupin to withdraw the 9th Light and the

---

1. This track as it ascends from below the eastern end of the brown hill is steep, narrow and winding, and is commanded from the slopes on each side.

47th from the trenches on the slopes falling towards Sare and the Col de St. Ignace, and place them in support of the 31st Light, whilst he himself went to the signal redoubt to encourage the garrison. After his arrival there he saw the 70th retiring from both the St. Ignace redoubts, and immediately sent orders to Taupin to retake the redoubts, repeating his intention to hold the right of the position. But, whilst the battle for the heights had been going on, the Light Division, which had concentrated on the Moniz plateau after the capture of the Petite Rhune works, had, in accordance with the plan, moved by degrees down towards the Col de St. Ignace under fire from Taupin's guns and infantry till it was spread under cover along the bank of the stream and its deep ravine, with the 52nd on its extreme left, where a narrow stone bridge crossed the stream about a mile below the actual col.[1]

Now that the trenches on the steep slopes in front of them were evacuated, came the chance of the division, and all along the line, Kempt's brigade on the right and Colborne's on the left, the advance commenced, and with cheers the skirmishers sprang up the slopes under fire from the redoubts above. But the 70th, shaken by the removal of the 9th and 47th, by the retirement of the other divisions, and the capture of the heights of Ascain by Freyre and Longa, evacuated the redoubts, fled in a panic and the divisional Commander heard nothing further of them till the next day; the Light Division then gained the heights, and advanced Kempt's to the south and Colborne with the 52nd to the north of the signal redoubt.

---

1. The present road from Sare to Ascain, which runs along the side of the long spur which descends towards Ascain, was not then in existence. The then track followed closely the bank of the stream in the ravine, on the right bank at first below the col, and then crossed by the bridge mentioned to the left bank, thence to Ascain. The time of the move from the Moniz is variously stated. Napier says 9.30 a.m., Kincaid, midday. Anyhow, it was not till after 11.30 a.m. that their final advance was made.

Meanwhile Taupin had reported to Clausel that he could not rally the 70th, and the latter realized that retreat was inevitable. Not wishing, however, to do so before he had made an effort to withdraw the 88th from the signal redoubt, he ordered Taupin to rally the 9th Light and 47th, the only remaining regiments of the division, and lead them to an attack on the Light Division to the west of the signal redoubt, whilst he with the 31st attacked to the east. But Taupin could not rally these regiments, already in retreat in a direction between Serres and Harosteguia, closely pursued by Kempt's brigade of Light Division. The 31st strongly engaged with the 4th Division in its front, its left flank threatened by the 7th and its right already turned by the Spanish, could not maintain its position, and also retreated towards the bridge of Harosteguia.

The signal redoubt had been invested by the 52nd soon after the advance of the Light Division, and Colborne had received an order from a staff officer, to take the redoubt, which order Baron Alten stated to Colonel Napier, he had not given or authorized. The 52nd suffered heavily when moving up against it, then made an attack on the redoubt which failed and Colborne withdrew the regiment to cover in a ravine close by. Again another attempt was made and again failed. Alten had already sent a staff officer to order Colborne not to renew the attack, but the bearer of it, Captain Harry Smith, had his horse shot under him, could not reach the regiment under the heavy fire from the redoubt, and had also to retire, "carrying off with his accustomed coolness his good and precious English saddle to the amusement of his observing friends and enemies."[1]

Now Colborne determined to try other means.

Making a bugler sound a parley, he hoisted his white handkerchief and rising walked round to the gate of the redoubt. To his summons, the old Chief (Commandant Gilles) replied, 'What! I with my battalion surrender to you with yours?'

1 Moorsom, *History of 52nd Regiment.*

'Very well!' said Colborne in French, 'Artillery will be soon up and you cannot hold out, and you will then be given over to the Spaniards'—some of whom were approaching.

The word 'Spaniards' was all-powerful; officers and men pressed round their Commander till he gave his reluctant consent. In a few minutes the 52nd stood formed in a double line at the gate of the redoubt to give the fine old fellow his required satisfaction of marching out with the honours of war. A detachment of the 52nd took the garrison down to Sare and handed them over to the cavalry."[1]

Whilst this was going on, the French in retreat were crossing the Nivelle. Conroux's division had crossed by the bridge at Olha, above St. Pée, but Maransin's division, which also made for this bridge, on reaching it found it held by the light troops of the 3rd Division, who, having crossed by the bridge of Amots and moved by the right bank of the river, were already in possession of the bridge at Olha and the village of St. Pée.

Maransin's division attempted to seize the bridge, but failed after a sharp contest, and had to turn about and cross by the bridges at Harosteguia and Urgury. Taupin's division was scattered; the 31st Light, followed by skirmishers of the 7th Division, crossed at Harosteguia, other regiments by fords opposite Helbarron, and the 47th which Taupin accompanied by the bridge at Ascain.

Though there was confusion no doubt, especially in Conroux's and Taupin's divisions, it should not be imagined that the French retreat towards the river was a flight or a rout. A competent witness, Lieut.-Colonel Frazer, R.H.A., in a letter written the next day thus states his opinion.

---

1. Napier. "The garrison had one man killed, whereas on the British side there fell 200 soldiers of a regiment never surpassed in arms, since arms were first borne by men."

On the whole the French did not show a determined spirit of resistance. Yet they fought like brave troops, but also like dispirited troops. There was no flight, nothing like a rout... they retired skirmishing.

And Lapene gives the same impression when he says, "All soon found themselves enveloped; it was no longer for victory that one fights, but to disengage."

After crossing the river Conroux's division had moved to the Habancen Borda works on the road from St. Pée to Ustaritz and Bayonne. Clausel, having rallied Maransin's division, and such regiments of Taupin's as had crossed near St. Pée, placed them on the high ground above and commanding the village. By about 2 p.m. all of Clausel's corps had crossed the river, being followed so far by parties of allied light troops.

Having gained possession of the Sare heights, Wellington stopped the advance for a short time to enable commands to be reformed and give the men a little rest, and then ordered the 3rd and 7th divisions to move to St. Pée, while the 4th, the Light and Giron's troops took up positions on the spurs running northwards from the heights and those facing Ascain to cover the movement from any interference from the enemy's troops about Serres.

At about 4 p.m. the advancing columns crossed the Nivelle by the bridges at Harosteguia and Urgury. At this time the French troops were endeavouring to recapture the village, then held by the light troops of the 3rd Division, but retired to the heights on arrival of the 3rd and 7th Divisions. When the 7th had crossed, Wellington sent it and Ross's troop, the only artillery which had come up, against the enemy. After a stiff fight, in which the 51st Regiment lost heavily—but gained Wellington's commendation in his dispatch—Maransin's division was driven from its position, and falling back to Habancen Borda joined Conroux's.

Darkness was now coming on, and this was the real ending of the attack by the centre, although the French, by

163

Clausel's order, kept up a desultory firing until about 8 p.m. with the object, he said, of "causing the enemy loss and of reviving the spirit of his troops." It was after 5 p.m. when Wellington heard that the 6th Division had arrived in the neighbourhood of St. Pée. The troops on both sides were weary after the long day's fighting. Those of the allied centre remained during the night in the positions they had seized.

CHAPTER 17

The Attack of the Right Wing

Before daybreak on the 10th of November Hill had placed; his divisions in the positions he considered "most eligible for their advance."[1] The country to be moved over is of the undulating foothill type, mostly open with heather, grass and gorse. In places it rises to over 500 feet, the general slope being from south to north towards the Sare basin, the average distance from Urdax to the French main position being about 4 miles.

On the left the 6th Division, under Sir H. Clinton, assembled "behind the hill on which the left piquet was posted," that is, on the left bank of the Nivelle, south of the frontier line and south-west of Dancharia. The Portuguese Division under Lieut.-General Sir H. Hamilton in rear of it on the road from Urdax, and the 2nd Division, under Sir W. Stewart, to the west of the hamlet of Landibar. Morillo's Spanish Division, whose task it was to cover the right flank of the corps during its advance by holding the French troops on the Chapora and Mondarrain heights, on the right rear between the river and these heights. As a further protection four battalions of Mina's troops [2] held the entrenchments which had been thrown up on the Gorospil heights to cover the right flank of the 6th Division when holding the Maya heights.

---

1. Hill's Report, Souraide, 11th November, 1813.
2. Mina's battalions were from 1,000 to 1,200 strong.

As directed in the instructions the advance was to be made in echelon of divisions from the left, and was commenced at about 6.30 a.m. by the 6th Division, Douglas's Portuguese brigade leading with an advanced guard of the 9th Cacadores and the light companies of Lambert's brigade under Lieut.-Colonel Brown of the 9th.

When the advanced guard had turned to the west the French post holding the ironworks called the forge d'Urdax, the main body of the division advanced, its direction point being the enemy's redoubt on the western end of the heights north of Ainhoa. As it moved forward the advanced guard drove the French from some buildings called by Clinton "the fortified house," its garrison retiring across the river.

As the division had also to cross, Colonel Brown was directed to find a suitable place, which he did in two fords concealed by a wood from the enemy's view. The division crossed, and Clinton was able to "place the troops at the very foot of the hill"[1] which was their objective.

Meanwhile the Portuguese Division, which had been moving along the left bank of the river, having driven the French post from the ironworks, had now also to cross, but some French light troops had collected on high ground which commanded the part of the river where Hamilton wished to pass. Seeing this, Clinton sent some companies of Lambert's brigade to menace the right of the French, who then retired from the right bank, and the Portuguese Division crossed by two fords; now it got into more difficult ground, having to cross the Ordokiso ridge, where it came under the fire of a battery placed on the northern slope of the Atchulegui mountain. Hamilton then halted the division until the Portuguese battery under Major Tulloh came up and "by a well-directed fire"[1] silenced the French guns; the division then moved on and descending into the ravine placed itself on the right of the 6th.

---

1. Clinton's Report. St. Pée, 11th November, 1813. 2. Hamilton's Report. Camp in front of Ainhoa, 11th November, 1813.

Whilst these moves were being made D'Erlon, seeing that Sare had been taken, and the rapid advance of the 3rd Division towards the heights above the bridge of Amots, ordered Darmagnac to put a stop to any kind of engagement in front of Ainhoa, and withdraw Chasse's brigade to the main position.

The 6th Division having reached the position from which it could launch its attack, which was to be made as soon as the Portuguese Division had taken up its position, Clinton ordered it to be carried out as follows—The advanced guard, having gained the enemy's right under cover of the wood skirting the foot of the hill, was to advance by the rocky spur which springs from the western end of the main ridge and drive the enemy's skirmishers from positions where they could bring a flanking fire against the attacking columns. These were to ascend the face of the hill on which the redoubt at point 669 stands, capture the redoubt and the defences about it. Lambert's brigade with the 12th Portuguese in first line covered by their light companies, with Pack's brigade and the 8th Portuguese in second line at a distance of 200 paces. To cover the right flank of these lines two companies of Lambert's brigade were to move up the wooded gorge on the attackers' right of the redoubt.

The 2nd Division, less Walker's brigade,[1] had assembled near Landibar, and driven off the French piquets on the right bank of the Aisaguerri stream and in front of Ainhoa. As soon as the 6th and Portuguese Divisions had crossed the Nivelle, the 2nd advanced in support of the Portuguese.

As soon as the Portuguese Division had reached "that point which would constitute the attack *en echelon*"[2] Clinton ordered the 6th to attack and both divisions advanced. The slopes were steep and progress hindered by thorn bushes, gorse, and the enemy's cross-fire from breastworks and trenches on the face of the hill caused severe losses in the first line; but the troops had no sooner reached the top of the ridge "than they rushed forward to

1. This brigade, which had just arrived after a forced march from Roncevaux, was by Hill's order detailed to support Morillo's division.
2. Clinton's report to Hill. Souraide, 11th November, 1813.

167

the assault of the redoubt, a square one with ditches of considerable depth."The French did not await the assault, but abandoned the redoubt and retreated rapidly along the heights, setting fire as they went to the hutted camp between the captured redoubt and the two on the hill (763) to the west of the Harismendia col.[1]

Hill now ordered the 6th and Portuguese Divisions to seize these two redoubts: the 6th changed front to the right and advanced eastwards along the ridge; but, fanned by the strong easterly wind, the huts burnt so fiercely that only two regiments were able to pass; Hamilton's division, which had reached the summit of the ridge opposite the lines of huts, was also hampered by the fire, but some units of his right brigade were to windward of it, and these with the two regiments of the 6th Division followed the French towards the two redoubts about point 763. On approaching them the French made a short stand, "but being pressed were driven from the hill and the redoubts were taken,"[2] with "even less resistance than the former."[3] Their garrisons joined the rest of Darmagnac's division, which, by D'Erlon's order, were now retreating by Amespetou towards Habancen, accompanied by the Corps Commander. As the guns in one of the redoubts had been left unspiked, one gun was, by Captain Brandreth's, R.A., exertions, brought into action against the retreating enemy.

When the 6th and Portuguese Divisions were in full possession of the right of the position held by Darmagnac's division, Sir William Stewart commanding the 2nd Division "deemed it advisable to direct Ashworth's Portuguese and Byng's brigades, covered by the light companies of the division under Major Ackland, 57th Regiment, against the enemy's position above Espelette"[4]—i.e. that part of the ridge to the east of the

1. Lapene. "Discouraged by this disaster—the rout of Conroux's division —Darmagnac's division only opposed a feeble resistance."
2. Hamilton's Report, 11th November, 1813.
3. Clinton's Report, 11th November, 1813.
4. Stewart's Report, 11th November, 1813. The light companies which were the first up suffered severely; every officer was wounded and Major Ackland killed.

col occupied by Boivin's brigade of Abbé's division—"The two brigades advanced against the position in very good style, as you witnessed, and carried the two redoubts on it in as spirited a manner as could be desired."

An eye-witness, Dr. Henry,[1] Surgeon of the 66th Regiment, thus describes this part of the action.

When the leading regiment of Byng's brigade reached the plateau at the top, it looked such a handful that a French column opposed to them deployed into line and prepared to charge, but, though I saw their officers cheering them on gallantly they would not advance, but kept up an irregular fire which did far less mischief than it ought to have done. When more force came up, and the brigade led by Byng formed and advanced in line, the enemy's line wavered—not metaphorically but, as I saw myself, visibly and materially, and, after two or three oscillations, they broke and ran.

There still remained a redoubt with two guns in possession of the enemy on the extreme left of their position (point 914); these were large ship carronades, and being loaded with double charges did much execution. Lieut.-Colonel Leith, 31st Regiment, Lieut.-Colonel Norton, 66th, and Ensign Dunne, 66th, at the head of a few men charged this work and carried it. Indeed, the three officers took it themselves, for they cleared the ditch with a running leap and dropped down amongst the garrison before a man could enter to assist them. As they leaped in, the artillery Officer and most of his men jumped out, but not with impunity, for Leith, a Hercules in figure and strength, knocked the red-headed Officer down with a brickbat; but his cap saved his skull, and he managed to scramble up and get away. His sergeant, a formidable-looking person,

---

1. W. Henry, *Events of a Military Life,* Chapter XVI.

'bearded like a pard,' was not so lucky; he dislocated his shoulder in the leap and was taken prisoner, and I set his arm to rights immediately afterwards.

Abbé, as testified by D'Erlon, "defended his ground with much bravery and obstinacy."[1] But now retreat was inevitable, and he withdrew the brigade to the heights above Espelette, where it was joined by Maucomble's brigade from the Atchulegui and Chapora heights, and the division then retired to the bridge-head at Cambo on the Nive.

When Darmagnac's division arrived at Habancen, D'Erlon, finding there the debris of Conroux's division, sent one of Darmagnac's brigades to Ustaritz to cover the road from Ainhoa to Bayonne, and himself accompanied it. On arrival he received a report from Abbé that the latter's division had taken up a position in advance of the Cambo bridge-head.

Whilst the three Anglo-Portuguese divisions were advancing towards the heights behind Ainhoa, Morillo's Spanish Division moving forward from the eastern end of the Maya ridge covered their right flank. When the main attack commenced Morillo engaged the brigade of Abbé's division which held the posts on the Chapora and Mondarrain heights, being supported by the 1st Brigade of the 2nd Division, which had the effect of holding the French brigade to its position. Indeed, Colonel Jones states, it caused D'Erlon to send troops from the right to their assistance.[2] Eventually Morillo was able to cut off some of Maucomble's brigade, and with part of his force drive them back towards Itxassou.

---

1. D'Erlon's Report to Soult, 11th of November.
2. Lieut.-Colonel J. T. Jones, R.E., *Account of War in Spain and Portugal and South of France:* "The blind confidence that Hill's attack would be directed along the ridge of mountains on their extreme left, which they carried to such a pitch that, whilst columns were absolutely in march to attack the position of Ainhoa, they were observed to be detaching troops from thence to their left."

The troops under Hill, less the 6th Division, which Wellington had ordered to move by the right bank of the Nivelle to St. Pée, bivouacked on the heights they had taken, after cavalry patrols had been sent towards Souraide and Espelette.

Towards evening Morillo's division, or part of it, arrived at the latter place, when they commenced to plunder and set fire to houses. A French woman having brought up this information, a British regiment and a squadron of 13th Light Dragoons was sent down to restore order, help to put out the fires and turn the Spaniards out of the village.[1]

FOY'S THREAT TO THE ALLIED RIGHT FLANK

General Foy with the 1st French Division at St. Jean Pied-de-Port had been separated from the main army ever since his divergent retreat from Sorauren on the 30th July. Later on he had been joined by Paris's brigade of the army of Aragon, which had moved into France from Jaca. On the 6th November Foy reported to Soult that Hill's corps had left the Roncevaux heights and moved to the Baztan valley being replaced by Mina's Spaniards. Soult, thereupon, ordered him to Bidarray, leaving at St. Jean only sufficient troops to man the entrenched camp, and also ordered the 1st Cavalry Division to move up to Cambo, and one brigade of the 2nd Division to St. Palais in support of the troops at St. Jean.

At Bidarray, where he arrived on the 8th November, Foy was in a position to defend the crossing of the Upper Nive there and at St. Martin d'Arossa if the enemy attempted to cut him off from St. Jean; and also by a movement towards the Gorospil mountain to act offensively against the enemy moving from the Maya heights against D'Erlon's position, or else to move to Espelette and reinforce D'Erlon.

---

1. Henry, *Events of a Military Life,* Ch. XVI, and *History of 13th Hussars.*

The orders given to Foy by the Marshal are thus stated in Soult's dispatch to the War Minister on the 11th November.

> Confident in the strength of the positions occupied by the army, I had previously ordered General Foy to reconnoitre the lines of advance from Bidarray towards the Gorospil in order that in case of an attack, and if he received the order to do so, he could advance against the right flank and rear of the enemy, a movement which would have produced a most useful diversion. Moreover, it was necessary to strongly cover the lines of advance towards Bidarray and St. Martin d'Arossa, by which the enemy could advance in strength and cut me off from St. Jean Pied-de-Port.

In this dispatch Soult also states that he had put Foy's division "at the disposition of D'Erlon." Whether Foy was informed of this remains uncertain. On the 9th, in accordance with his instructions, Foy reconnoitred the country towards the Gorospil, in the neighbourhood of which camps were visible.

At 7 a.m. on the 10th Foy received an order from D'Erlon, sent at midnight on the 9th, to send one of his brigades to Espelette. But Foy, always independent, put the order in his pocket and determined to carry out the operation he had planned for himself; and, leaving his men's knapsacks at Bidarray, moved, on hearing the first sound of gunfire, towards the Gorospil. His reasons for so acting, as given in his journal, were that owing to the distance and the difficult country between Bidarray and Espelette, he considered compliance with the order would be not only useless, but would reduce his strength to the advantage of neither party.[1]

On approaching the Gorospil ridge he found Mina's battalions there, and having dislodged one from the heights, he attacked with Fririon's brigade; and in spite "of bravery wor-

---

1. Girod de l'Ain, *Journal du General Foy.*

thy of better troops" drove them back to the pass of Maya and down into the Baztan valley. Here he came upon some of the baggage of Grant's cavalry brigade, all of which was captured, including a Paymaster and his treasure chest.[1]

Now it became evident to Foy from the direction and the increasing distance of the firing, that the French were re-treating, and that to save his division he must at once retreat, so he moved back to Bidarray, where his men picked up their knapsacks, and, having placed posts on the Nive there and at St. Martin, he, following his orders in case of retreat, marched to Cambo where the division arrived during the night of 10th/11th November.

The flank guard of Mina's battalions, though driven from their position, finely performed their duty in so much as they contained for the best part of the day an entire division of Soult's army. Foy's tribute to their bravery is honourable both to him and to them.

---

1. Hope, *Military Memoirs.* "It was related at the time, and very generally credited, that if common prudence and exertion had been used, not a part of the baggage would have fallen into the hands of the French." Wellington shared this view, for he refused to approve of any claims for compensation on the ground that his orders regarding the security of the baggage of the army had not been complied with.

CHAPTER 18

Analysis of the Battle

About two months after the battle Colonel H. Bunbury, the Under-Secretary for War, was sent by the Cabinet to Wellington's Headquarters at St. Jean de Luz—

> to explain to him more fully than could be done by letters, the extreme difficulty the Government found in complying with his urgent and repeated calls for money and provisions; to ascertain his wishes as to the extent of the supplies required, and the ports where they should' be landed, also to give him the latest information regarding the hopes and desires of the allied Powers.

In his Memoirs[1] Bunbury states that one evening at dinner he took the liberty of asking Wellington the following question: "Which of his victories he considered the best in plan and execution." His answer was, "Well, I think the battle of the Nivelle was my best work."

Though on a very small scale and with little artillery action on the part of the Allies, this battle has some of the characteristics of the great engagements of the last war. For a month both sides had faced each other in close contact, and both had dug themselves in. The possession of the Great Rhune with its wide field of view gave the Allies some superiority of position; but the French had quite sufficient view from their positions to

---

1. *Memoir of Sir H. Bunbury, Bt.* Edited by his son.

be able to locate the dispositions of the allied troops. The early issue of the plan of attack to corps and divisional commanders gave them time to study the ground and make their dispositions accordingly. The plan itself was simple, and the lines of advance clearly laid down; the rest was left to the subordinate commanders. The results obtained were creditable to them, their staffs, and all ranks serving under them. Wellington did not exaggerate when he termed it good work.

Though simple, the plan was masterly. The constant reconnaissance of the French positions by Wellington personally and by his staff, as well as the information of movements regularly received from divisions, had disclosed the strong and the weak points in the enemy's position. He had early seen that the strongly entrenched position in front of St. Jean de Luz, which had behind it a tidal river, was not the point to be chosen to make a break in the French line.[1]

The weak point was found in the gap of Amots, which was weak in its physical features, and as being the point of junction of two commands, those of Clausel and of D'Erlon.

Towards success in war the influence and personality of the Leader have ever been dominant factors. "It was Caesar who conquered Gaul, and not the Roman legions," said Napoleon, and the same might be said of himself. In action it was Wellington's custom to be in such close contact with his troops as would not be possible for a chief commander now. What this meant he once explained as follows—

When I come myself the soldiers think that what they have to do is the most important since I am there, and that all depends on their exertions. Of course these are increased in proportion, and they will do for me what, perhaps, no one else can make them do.[2]

---

1. Wellington to Bathurst, St. Pée, 13th November, 1813. "The enemy, not satisfied with the natural strength of this position, had the whole of it fortified; and their right in particular had been made so strong that I did not deem it expedient to attack it in front."
2. *Larpent's Journal.*

By the plan Wellington concentrated greatly superior strength on all important points of the enemy's line. Every available man was put in. One Portuguese brigade formed his only general reserve, each division having to provide its own. Napier's final comment on the battle aptly states the cause of the French defeat, thus, "Lord Wellington directed superior numbers with superior skill."

As has been stated previously the plan, if successful, contained the possibility of a great victory. How was it that this was not gained? To the answer quoted as having been given by Wellington to Colonel Bunbury at the dinner table must be added the following statement made on the same occasion. "If I could have trusted the Spaniards[1] for two hours—if they could have been brought only to hold their ground—I would have obliged the whole of Soult's right wing to lay down their arms." Wellington here was evidently referring to the menace to the left flank and communications of his centre corps by the presence at Serres of Darricau's division and Saint Pol's Italian brigade of Villatte's division, a total of about 8,000 men. He may also have received information from the look-out officers on the Great Rhune of the movement towards Serres of the remainder of Villatte's division which Gleig says was noticed towards 3 p.m. It was this menace, and it was a very real one, for the whole of the baggage, transport and supply of the centre divisions would have to pass by Sare and its neighbourhood, that led Wellington to leave the 4th,[2] the Light, and Giron's corps on the left bank of the river ready to support Freyre and Longa, who held the ground opposite Serres which commanded the bridge at Ascain.

If Wellington had felt confident that Freyre and Longa could, and would, hold their ground, he would, as his answer to Bunbury implies, have pushed forward across the river with

---

1. Freyre's and Longa's divisions holding the ground about Ascain.
2. B. Smyth, *A History of Lancashire Fusiliers, 20th Regt. (4th Division).* "The Regiment was still following the French, who had taken to the bridges over the Nivelle, when it was halted by Lord Wellington."

four divisions instead of two, and, without waiting for the 6th Division, have advanced so as to command the St. Jean de Luz-Bayonne and other roads in that direction, and thereby cut the line of retreat of Reille's corps. Not being sure of the Spaniards, he did not feel justified in taking the risk.

The question now arises why was it that the 6th Division did not arrive in the neighbourhood of St. Pée until after 5 p.m.? It is not easy to find an answer. On the next day Wellington at St. Pée wrote to Hope as follows—

> Everything succeeded as I wished, except the length of time which our different operations took. Notwithstanding that we began at daylight it was one o'clock before I could put in motion the troops on the right of the Nivelle, and they had not arrived in this neighbourhood at five o'clock. If we could have moved forward from hence early yesterday Soult could not have retired easily from St. Jean de Luz.

Beyond stating the time when their commands advanced, none of the corps or divisional commanders in their reports on the battle give the time at which any phase of their proceedings during the day took place. For any information regarding time reference has to be made to the French commanders' reports, and statements by eye-witnesses such as Napier, Frazer and others. As regards the 6th Division, D'Erlon's report makes no mention of any time, and with one exception,[1] such regimental histories as exist of the British units of the division make no mention of times and give no information regarding their movements after the attack on the right of D'Erlon's position.

---

1. *Historical Records of 91st Highlanders, 6th Division.* "The allied troops by their impetuosity swept everything in front of them, the 6th Division crossed the river about 7 a.m. some distance above Amots, and by the right bank threatened the bridge (this time is probably that of crossing by the advanced guard), driving the French out of the partially finished fort covering the bridge, and then turning to the right drove Darmagnac's division through the hutted camp towards Habancen Borda."

In the letter already quoted Wellington specifies "the troops on the right of the Nivelle." Undoubtedly, he refers to some of those under Hill's command, but it cannot refer to all of them because the whole of Hill's original command, the 2nd Division, the Portuguese Division and that of Morillo, did not advance on that day beyond the captured position, cavalry patrols only being sent out towards Souraide and Espelette. It must therefore refer to the 6th Division,[1] which had come under Hill's command on the previous day. But from Wellington's letter already quoted, the further inference has been drawn that it was not till 1 p.m. that Hill's attack on D'Erlon's position commenced.[2]

It would appear, however, that this inference is not correct for the following reasons. In his report Clinton states—

the active intelligence of Lieutenant-Colonel Brown enabled me to place the troops (6th Division) destined to make the attack on the right of the enemy at the very foot of the hill; as I observed, however, the extreme difficulties of the ground prevented Lieutenant-General Hamilton's Portuguese Division from making the same progress and that the enemy was still in possession of the high ground commanding that part of the river where he intended to cross, I sent two companies of Lambert's brigade supported by the 12th Portuguese Regiment to menace the enemy's right; as soon as the object of this move was attained, the dispositions for the principal attack was made. . . . As soon as Lieutenant-General Hamilton's division had by considerable exertions arrived at that point which would constitute an attack in echelon, I ordered the 6th Division to attack.

1. Hope, *Military Memoirs*. "About 10 a.m. on the 11th the 2nd Division quitted the heights from which they had driven the enemy the previous day."
2. Vidal de la Blache, *L'Evacuation d'Espagne,* Vol. I. "They (Hill's Corps) did not attack until the skirmishers of the 3rd Division had crossed by the bridge of Amots to the right bank and turned Darmagnac's right. It was then one o'clock."
Fortescue, *History of the British Army,* Vol. X. "Soon after 1 p.m. Hill launched his troops to the attack."

In his report Hamilton says—

We crossed a deep ravine, ascended and gained the fortified height at the enemy's huts between the two forts, at the same time as that on our left was carried by the 6th Division.

With these reports as a basis and following the advances of these divisions, it is possible to arrive at the approximate time at which the attack commenced. At daybreak the 6th Division was assembled behind the hill north of Urdax held by the left piquet of its outposts. Sending forward an advanced guard of 9th Cacadores and the light companies of Lambert's brigade, the main body of the division advanced at 6.30 a.m. From the assembly point of the division to where it crossed the Nivelle is 2½ miles. If the rate of marching is put at two and a half miles an hour, the river would be reached at 7.30 a.m., and the division be over at 8.10 a.m.[1] From there to "the foot of the hill" is about one mile over more difficult ground, the head of the division was at the foot of the hill at about 8.40 a.m. and the whole division up at about 9.20 a.m.[2] The main body met with no opposition during the march; what little there was the advanced guard had disposed of.

The Portuguese Division started from about the same point as the 6th, but half an hour later, and had about the same distance to cover. As far as the river the division met with little opposition as the French party holding the ironworks retired on the approach of the advanced guard. But on reaching the river, about half a mile higher up than where the 6th Division had crossed, there was considerable delay until the troops sent by Clinton obliged the French to retire. Having forded the river at about 8.40 a.m.,

---

1. Napier says "the 3rd Division was encouraged by the rapid advance of the 6th."

2. Dumas, *Neuf mois de Campagne á la suite du Maréchal Soult.* "The troops put in movement by Hill arrived about 9 o'clock in front of the position on D'Erlon's right," and adds in a note, "All the French reports indicate 9 or 9.30 a.m."

there was further delay when crossing the Ordokiso heights until the Portuguese battery came up and was able to deal with the French guns which were shelling the heights. Considering these delays and the difficult ground to be traversed after crossing the Nivelle, it is probable that the Portuguese Division did not come into position until about 10.15 a.m., and that the simultaneous attack by it and the 6th began about 10.30 a.m.[1]

When D'Erlon withdrew all his troops which had opposed Hill's advance, and had assembled Darmagnac's division on the right of his position, Lapene tells us that—

> it was scarcely in line when they saw the left of Clausel's position being evacuated and that their right and rear were being threatened by the troops which had defeated Conroux's division" (i.e. the 3rd British division). Discouraged by this combination of mishaps, Darmagnac's division put up only a feeble resistance, when the allies, already in occupation of Ainhoa, attacked in formidable strength.

Hope says—

> The contest was severe, but not very long, for the enemy seeing the British were determined to bear down all opposition retired from their strongholds one after another, and at length, making a virtue of necessity, finally left the heights.

The following extracts from the statements of actual observers seem to show that this time is at any rate approximately correct.

---

1. Since the above was written the *Peninsular Journal* of Major-General Sir Benjamin Durban has been published. On the 10th November, 1813, he writes as follows: "The whole of the front of the enemy's position from Sare inclusive to the Nivelle attacked by the centre corps was in our possession by 10.30 a.m. Meanwhile, or very shortly after, the Light Division on the left and the 6th Division and Sir R. Hill's Corps on the right, respectively, carried their points of attack and before 12 o'clock the enemy was everywhere completely beaten and in full retreat."

In his dispatch describing the battle, Wellington writes—

The whole then co-operated in the attack of the enemy's position behind Sare. The 3rd and 7th Divisions carried the redoubts on the left of the enemy's centre. . . . Whilst these operations were being carried out I had the pleasure to see the 6th Division make a most handsome attack on the right of the enemy's position behind Clinton and carry all their entrenchments.[1]

Now it is agreed in all accounts that by n a.m. all the ground between the Louis XIV redoubt and the Nivelle was in possession of the 3rd and 7th Divisions. The Commissariat[2] officer says—

Whilst the 3rd Division was thus engaged with Conroux's division, the 6th Division was storming the redoubts at that point of the line north of Ainhoa.

Major Hope[3] (92nd, 2nd Division) writes—

The first operations of the army were completely hid from our vision, but by degrees the tide of battle began to roll towards us, and by 10 o'clock the battle had begun to rage with considerable fury all along almost every part of the enemy's line.

From these statements it may be assumed that Darmagnac's division was in retreat about noon, followed, as Napier states, by the 6th Division.

Hill's instructions state clearly that he was to establish himself securely "on the ground gained, and wait there for fresh instructions in regard to his further movements."[4] By whom then was the order given which sent the 6th Division in pursuit of that of Darmagnac? The question is one which it seems impossible to answer definitely.

---

1. Wellington to Bathurst, St. Pée, 13th November, 1813.
2. *Journal of a Commissariat Officer* (attached to 3rd Division).
3. Hope, *Military Memoirs*.
4. Q.M.G. to Hill, 27th October, 1813.

It does not seem likely that the order was given by Hill on his own responsibility. There was no man in that army more loyal to his chief, less self-assertive, or likely to act contrary to his instructions unless circumstances obliged him to do so. We know, indeed, that on the 31st July, when following the French after Sorauren, he changed his line of advance from that in his orders, and that his doing so was freely acknowledged by Wellington as having been correct.[1] But here there was no urgent need for him to do so. To ascertain the direction of Darmagnac's retreat all that was necessary was to follow him by cavalry as Hill's orders directed him to do. Indeed, the direction taken by Darmagnac must have been clearly seen from the captured ridge. If not given by Hill the order must have come from the army headquarters, or by Clinton on his own responsibility. By whomsoever the order was given, it had a fatal effect on the complete success of the day. The prime need the situation required was that Wellington should have in hand sufficient strength to enable him to move from St. Pée as early in the day as possible if he was to have a fair chance of cutting off the retreat of Reille's two divisions from St. Jean de Luz.

There appears to be no trace of any order on the subject from Wellington's headquarters. There is the 1 p.m. order mentioned in Wellington's dispatch on the battle; but this states definitely that the 6th Division was to advance by the right bank of the river; no mention is made of the following up of the enemy by this division.

It may be that as the 6th Division. was pushing Darmagnac along the ridge and down through the Col de Harismendia it continued to follow without any reference to the higher command, in which case Sir H. Clinton must be held responsible.

It is unfortunate that there appears to be no definite information on the point or as regards the movements of the

---

1. Wellington to the Conde de la Bispal, 1st August, 1813. "The case was one of those in which it is obligatory on a General in his Chief's confidence to depart from his orders."

6th Division after it left the French position. Had the division been on the heights when the 1 p.m. order arrived, it could have reached St. Pée by the Col de Harismendia and Amespetou by about 3.30 p.m. It seems clear that the fact of the division following Darmagnac was the cause of its failure to arrive at St. Pée too late, and that it thus helped to save the French right wing.

The Anglo-Portuguese casualties during the action were—killed, wounded and missing, 184 officers and 2,441 other ranks.

THE FRENCH SIDE

To Soult's surprise and alarm his entrenched line had failed him. It did so for several reasons. It was too long for the number of troops available to hold it, consequently it was thin and weak everywhere; so many men were, required to hold the front that few were left for local support. With such a line the French dared not concentrate any considerable body for counter-attack, or to reinforce any specially threatened point.

Soult's distribution of his force was bad. Clinging from the first to the assumption that the allied attack would be made against his right, he apparently neglected to consider what clues might be gathered from the distribution of the allied forces, and where the weak points in his own line were.

Both his own position and that of his general reserve were wrongly placed; with the consequence that he had no personal influence over the course of the battle; and his general reserve, placed behind the strongest and best-manned part of his line, never came into action at all.

In his dispatch of 19th November, 1813, to the War Minister, Soult thus stated what may be considered his sort of apologia for the defeat of his army.

Before the attack I would not have believed that the divisions of General Clausel could have been driven from the positions behind Sare and on the Petite Rhune which they had to defend. Such happenings are beyond the laws of probabilities. The enemy should have lost 25,000 men in capturing them. I can only regret they were so cheaply won after all the labour we have given to render them impregnable.

Words little generous to his army, the greater part of which did fight well.

In a memorandum written on the day of the battle, Colonel Michaud, one of the ablest men in the army, gives his opinion why the battle was lost. It is a frank criticism of the Marshal's action. He says—

The distribution of the enemy's troops during the last eight days[1] has shown that his intention was to attack the centre of the French army about Sare, and to demonstrate only against other points. Whilst Wellington was preparing for the attack no change was made in the distribution of the French army.[2] The right was so strong holding a short line strongly entrenched and forming a double obstacle (with the river behind it) that it ought to have been clear that the enemy would not make his effort on that side.

The centre held a much longer line, the entrenchments were in an unfinished state; and, if this position was captured all the works on the left bank of the Nivelle as far as St. Jean de Luz would fall without being attacked; and the enemy be able to advance without any further

1. His statement of the allied distribution is not quite correct, but sufficiently so to prove the correctness of his conclusions. Colonel Michaud was the chief Field Engineer; from the nature of his duties he had an intimate knowledge of the ground and adjacent country.
2. Soult to Guerre, 8th November, 1813. "Whilst waiting (for the attack) I am always ready to give battle, and I maintain the dispositions I have ordered."

obstacle either on Cambo, or Ustaritz or Bayonne. Everything therefore pointed to his moving against Amots as his first offensive movement. The left held a good position well entrenched, but D'Erlon's force was insufficient to man all the works constructed. The enemy knew the weak points in our position. One has always thought that the right of the army was held in too great strength, and that the reserve divisions ought to have been placed at St. Pée and Amots; also that when it was known that the enemy was concentrating about Vera, in the Baztan valley and leaving Roncevaux, Foy's division should have been moved to Espelette, and not left to *'faire le partizan'* on the rear of the enemy's army.[1]

One cannot doubt the justice of most of the Colonel's conclusions.

It has been said that the great soldier, whose recent death has been mourned in both France and the British Empire, believed that success in the field of battle depends mainly on two things, the moral factor and the influence of the Commander.[2] So what of the moral of the army under Soult, and of his influence over it? The Marshal was one whose written word cannot be taken always as the truth and the whole truth. Though he constantly endeavoured to impress the War Minister and the Emperor that the moral of his army was satisfactory, he must have been aware that all was not well with it. From the time of the retreat into France after Soult's unsuccessful attempt to relieve Pamplona the confidence of the army in its Chief, and in itself, had diminished, Soult's capacity as a leader in the field was challenged.[3] The subsequent constant defeats, together with the hardships the army had undergone owing to scanty food, little pay, and the severity of the weather, had further diminished its moral.

---

1. That it did so was partially caused by Foy's disobedience of orders.
2. *The Times,* 21st March, 1929.
3. Vidal de la Blache, *L'Evacuation de l'Espagne.* *"Les troupes répondaient au dépit de leur chef par des sentiments tout pareils."*

In this particular action, stretched out over a long line, tied down to fixed positions, everywhere attacked by superior numbers, and nowhere supported by adequate reserves, it is little wonder that the rank and file, seeing the line broken elsewhere and their flanks threatened, should become discouraged. That good soldier, Clausel, other generals and most of the officers were game to the last, but they could not hold their men. Nor did they receive any assistance from their Chief either in the shape of reinforcements or from his personal presence. Except perhaps on the right, where he was not wanted, he did not appear on the field during the day.

This raises another disputed point in connection with the battle. Where did Soult place himself during the day? Lapène says: "Since the commencement of the battle the General-in-Chief and his staff had arrived at the extremity of the camp of Serres, so as to be in touch with his line -and the phases of the action." General Dumas[1] shows why Lapene is not to be depended on in any statements affecting Soult personally, because his book, published in 1823, was written under the influence of Soult. He is of the opinion that all documents agree that Soult did not arrive at Serres until about 4 p.m. when the battle was over.

Captain Vidal de la Blache states that Soult, after sending a letter at about 10.30 a.m. to General Thouvenat at Bayonne, which was headed *"au bivouac en avant de St. Jean de Luz,"* went to Villatte's reserve division on the hill of Serres. But the following extracts from Soult's dispatches to the War Minister appear to confirm General Dumas' opinion.

Serres, 10th November, 1813. This morning at daybreak the army was attacked along the whole line. Maucune's and Boyer's divisions and that of Villatte, who were on the right where I was, and Darricau's, which was on the heights of Serres, have perfectly defended their positions.

---

1. *Neuf mois de campagne a la suite du Maréchal Soult.*

Bayonne, 19th November. I could not foresee that I would not have time to arrive to the assistance of these divisions (Clausel's). I could only judge what was happening on the left from the direction of the firing, as no reports reached me. However, I arrived at the reserve in time to prevent the enemy launching his troops in pursuit of Clausel, and stop the movement of two British divisions advancing on his right and crossing the Nivelle below Ibarron.

It thus seems clear that Soult and the general reserve under Villatte remained about St. Jean de Luz until the afternoon, and their movement towards Serres was that noticed by Gleig at about 3 p.m. But Serres was not the place for the General-in-Chief or his reserve. From the commencement of the action both should have been between St. Pée and Amots, as suggested by Colonel Michaud.

In his report, when dealing with the last phase of the action, Clausel says he "expected to see the arrival of the reserves from Serres." The troops there under Darricau were not a reserve in the real sense of the term. Darricau, no doubt under Soult's orders, had a definite task to fulfil, namely to link the centre with the right wing, and to prevent the enemy thrusting a force between the right of Clausel's position and the river thereby turning his right. Had Darricau moved up on to Clausel's position, the way would have been open for Freyre and Longa to move right round it and join hands with Beresford's corps.

The French casualties during the battle were, killed, wounded and prisoners: officers, 174; other ranks, 4,270; of whom 27 officers and 1,231 other ranks were prisoners of war.

CHAPTER 19

The Retreat of the French Army

Driven from the centre of his position behind Sare and also from that behind Ainhoa, also, with the fact before him, that several divisions of the allied army were across the Nivelle about St. Pée, and therefore in a position to intercept the retreat towards Bayonne of Reille's corps and the troops at Serres, whilst the direct road from St. Pée to Bayonne (10 miles) was open to the enemy, Soult could do nothing else but order a general retreat northwards.

His views on the situation are best given in his own words written at Serres to the War Minister on the evening of the 10th. He says—

I propose to-morrow to take up a position, the right at Bidart, and the left at Arrauntz—a front of about 6 miles. It is possible, however, that I shall not halt there, but continue the movement to Bayonne, where I shall have sufficient troops to occupy the entrenched camp, and with the rest of the army take up a position on the right bank of the Nive and holding the Ursouia mountain. There I shall be midway between Bayonne and St. Jean Pied-de-Port, and so cover both places. The enemy's strength is so great that I cannot hold such extensive positions as I have done in order to cover the country, therefore I am going to concentrate and manoeuvre as an army. Keeping the troops together and constantly under my eye, their moral will be better, and the enemy will be obliged also to keep his troops more together.

In accordance with this decision orders were sent to Reille[1] to place Boyer's and Leval's divisions on the heights of Bidart to cover "the great road" to Bayonne. He was to send immediately all the field artillery and the greater part of his troops across the Nivelle, leaving detachments only in the principal works, who were to spike such position guns and destroy such munitions as they could not carry off. They were also to destroy the bridge between St. Jean de Luz and Ciboure[2] and the trestle bridge higher up the river, as soon as the last of the destruction parties had crossed the river.

By 6 a.m. on the 11th Reille's two divisions and the artillery had crossed the river, having left a rear-guard at Guethary to bring on the destruction parties; the divisions arrived at Bidart at 9 a.m. Orders to retire had also been issued to the other corps. Darricau's division to Arbonne, Maransin's, Taupin's and Conroux's from Habancen to Arcangues. Of D'Erlon's corps, Darmagnac's division had already returned to Ustaritz, and Abbé's to Cambo, where it was joined by that of Foy during the night 10th to 11th. The Marshal with Villatte's division proceeded also to Arcangues.

Thus on the 11th the French army was in the position indicated in Soult's dispatch of the 10th. It had effected its retreat without any interference from the allied army. But at about 2 p.m. the heads of several allied columns showed themselves. General and staff officers were seen reconnoitring, and there was some firing by the outposts.

It was apparent to Soult that a general engagement on the next day was inevitable if he remained where he was; to avoid it he decided to again retire. Writing to the War Minister on the 11th he thus states his reasons.

---

1. Gazan to Reille, Serres, 10th November.
2. This bridge carried the main road; it was of wood and in two parts which connected an island in the river with both banks.

Although I am disposed to give battle, it appears to me that my present position is not the best one I can take up. It is still too extensive as compared with the forces the enemy can bring against me, therefore I am about to issue orders for the army to take up a position to-morrow on the plateau of Beyris between Anglet and the Nive. If the enemy attacks me I will give him battle even if his strength is double mine. I have decided to defer the movement to the right bank of the Nive in order to keep the enemy in view and hinder movements, and also to get the work on the entrenched camp finished under my own eyes.[1]

On the same day he wrote to the Governor of Bayonne—

I will remain in the position held by the army as long as possible in order to give you time to finish the works of the entrenched camp. But at any moment I may be obliged to retire on Bayonne, so you must have everything ready for its defence and see to the inundations.[2]

The French retired during the night 11th to 12th, leaving rear-guards which were to follow at daybreak. The positions to be occupied in front of Bayonne were as follows. Reille's two divisions were to be placed across the main road in front of the village of Anglet. Clausel's corps to prolong this line to the left along the high ground above the stream which flows into the Brindos lake, on its left D'Erlon was to place Darmagnac's division across the Bayonne-Ustaritz-St. Jean Pied-de-Port road with Abbé's division in rear of it as support. Darricau's and Villatte's divisions to be in reserve on the plateau of Beyris in rear of the centre.

But, whilst this move was being carried out, Soult again changed his plan, and decided to place Reille's and Clausel's corps in the immediate vicinity of Bayonne to hold the two entrenched camps outside the fortress which had been thrown

1. Soult to Guerre, Arcangues, 11th November, 1813.
2. Soult to Thouvenot, 11th November, 1813.

up, namely the Spanish front camp between the Adour River below the town and the Nive, and that of Mousserolles between the Nive and the Adour, and, using the bridges in the city, to place D'Erlon's corps on the right bank of the Nive to support Foy at Cambo and prevent any attempt the allied army might make to cross that river. To secure unity of command on that bank, he placed Foy's division, P. Soult's cavalry division and Paris's brigade at Bidarray on the upper Nive under D'Erlon's command.

This decision would appear to have been made by Soult as soon as he was assured that he was not being closely followed by the allied army. Until he was certain of this he could not afford to make any detachments, being liable to attack at any moment by superior forces; but, once close up to the defence works, he appears to have been satisfied he could hold them with the corps of Reille and Clausel. And probably he foresaw that the possession of the bridge over the Nive within the town might be very useful in the future.

The unprotected state of the right bank of the Nive, as it would have been under his original plan, was a real danger he had to meet; and the information he received during the day regarding the allied movement towards Cambo and Ustaritz confirmed it. Its possession by the enemy would give the latter more freedom of manoeuvre, whilst restricting his. It would sever his communications with St. Jean Pied-de-Port and give the allies the use of the road from Bayonne to that place, the only good one on the right bank, and access to the interior of France whence he could draw some supplies and intelligence. Moreover, if the enemy gained the left bank of Adour above Bayonne he would be in a position to restrict, if not stop, all the water traffic on that river, by which, owing to the bad state of the roads on the right bank, the greater part of supplies and munitions for the French army, as well as food for the inhabitants, reached Bayonne.

On the evening of the 12th November the French army was distributed as follows. Reille's corps about Anglet and on the Beyris plateau covering the main road; Clausel's corps on Reille's left in front of the entrenched camp of Marrac with its left on the Nive; Villatte's division in rear of Clausel. The three divisions of D'Erlon's corps had crossed the Nive, and were placed, Abbé's division at Vieux Mougerre in front of the Mousserolles defences between the Nive and the Adour, Darmagnac's division at Villefranque, Darricau at Halsou, Foy at Cambo, P. Soult's cavalry division at Urcuray and Hasparren on the then main road from Bayonne to St. Jean Pied-de-Port.

CHAPTER 20

The Advance of the Allied Army

The divisions of the army passed the night 10th/11th November in the positions they had reached on the evening I of the 10th. Hill's corps, less the 6th Division, on the heights north of Ainhoa, the 3rd and 7th Divisions about St. Pée, with the 6th on their right; the 4th and Light with Giron's Spaniards on the left bank of the Nivelle overlooking Serres and Ibarron. Freyre's corps about Ascain and Hope's about Urrugne and in front of Ciboure. Wellington's headquarters were at St. Pée.

When the battle was over it was evident that Soult must either retire northwards or stand to fight again. If he retreated there was still the possibility of intercepting Reille's corps: so on the evening of the 10th orders were sent to Hope and Freyre to cross the Nivelle as early as possible on the 11th. Hope was told to press the rear of the French as closely as possible if they retired so as to prevent them destroying the bridges over the river, and he was to establish quickly pontoon bridges. When his troops had crossed he was to advance to Guethary and take up a position on the heights there. Freyre was to occupy the heights behind Ahetze, but his left column was to extend along the right bank of the river as far as the tile works about a mile up stream from St. Jean de Luz.

Hill, on the right, was to place his troops across the heights facing Souraide and covering the Ainhoa-Espelette road. He was to observe Cambo and Ustaritz, and be in communication with the divisions of the centre of the army. The centre of the army was to advance on the 11th and take up a position beyond the Bois de St. Pée facing towards Bayonne, the movement being made in two columns. That on the right the 3rd and 7th Divisions, followed by Giron's corps; the left column composed of the 4th and Light Divisions and Bradford's Portuguese brigade. Each column had with it a cavalry regiment and artillery. The 6th Division was to be on the right of the army, and to move parallel to the 3rd and 7th Divisions.

As Hope had not been able to prevent serious damage being done by the French to the Ciboure-St. Jean de Luz town bridge, and to the trestle bridge higher up the river, he could not advance in force on the nth until the pontoon bridges were laid, and the tide had fallen sufficiently to make the fords practicable, which on that day was about noon. Batty thus describes the crossings.

> About half-past twelve the columns of the 5th Division and the second brigade of Guards passed the Nivelle, part by fords close above the town, and part with artillery over the bridge. The 1st Division with Wilson's Portuguese brigade by a ford about a mile higher up the river. It rained in torrents the whole forenoon.[1]

In order that the advance might be made in a general line, that of the centre corps had also to be postponed till Hope had crossed. His advanced guard reached Guethary about 2 p.m., and the corps bivouaced on the heights which extend from the sea near that village to the south of Ahetze. By nightfall the centre had come into line and the two corps were within striking distance of that taken up by the French, from Bidart by Arbonne, Arcangues, Ste. Barbe to Arraunts.

Such being the position Wellington on the evening of the 11th wrote to Hope as follows—

---

1. Batty, *Campaign of Western Pyrenees*. The bridge he refers to must have been one of the pontoon bridges as the town bridge was not sufficiently repaired to carry artillery till the following day.

I think it is probable they will retire tonight. If they do not, I propose to attack them tomorrow morning about 10 o'clock, and will send you the plan as soon as I see their position at daylight. It appears to me we must move from the right of our centre upon the left of their position at Ste. Barbe, always keeping our right forward so as to fall upon their communications with Bayonne.

There was a dense fog on the morning of the 12th. Covered by this and making a very early start the French retired to close to the Bayonne defences. When the fog cleared the allied left and centre advanced, and in the evening were on a line from Bidart, by the heights of Baroillet and Arcangues.

On the 11th Hill was instructed to make a move towards the River Nive on the 12th. If he found the French disposed to yield the defences he had on the left bank of that river, or if he could be forced from them without engaging in a serious affair, he was told Wellington desired him to drive them across the river; but his chief operations were to be against Cambo, that being the principal passage held by the French opposite Hill's front. He was also directed to send some troops to Ustaritz, and to obtain as much information as possible about the river[1] and the enemy's defences.

On the evening of the 11th the French troops in front of Hill retired towards Cambo, and Hill followed them to within about 3 miles from that village and bivouacked in heavy rain. On the 12th, Hill, having sent detachments to Ustaritz and Larressore, and reconnoitring patrols along the river above and below Cambo, again advanced about midday with the 2nd Division. His left column, composed of the 2nd and 3rd brigades, moved first towards the river and when within a few hundred yards wheeled half right and advanced against Cambo. The 1st brigade on the right moved by the Ainhoa-Espelette road, and pushing back the

---

1. Q.M.G. to Hill, St. Pée, 11th November, 1813.

enemy's piquets to a short distance from their works, turned to the right and ascended an eminence which overlooked the town and the whole of the enemy's defences within artillery range.

> Here Sir Rowland reconnoitred the French, when, finding them better prepared for us than was expected, he contented himself with driving back their light troops and cannonading the garrison. In the evening we retired about a mile and encamped.[1]

The rain which had commenced on the 11th November continued to fall without ceasing until the 16th, consequently the so-called roads were knee-deep in mud, the rivers in full flood, and the streams swollen into broad and deep rivers. Writing to Sir W. Clinton on the 14th Wellington said—

> The state of the roads and the shortness of the day prevented me from doing all I wished, and the enemy was enabled to retire on Bayonne. The weather is so bad and the Spanish troops in such distress, I am afraid I can do no more at present.

The Spaniards, being in such a state, it is hardly surprising that want led to plunder and other mischief.[2] But Wellington would have none of this; everything, he said, "depended on our moderation" and gaining the confidence of the inhabitants, and therefore he sent the Spaniards back into cantonments in their own country. This commenced on the 13th: Giron's Andalusians to the Bastan valley; Longa to Medina in the Ebro valley; Freyre to Irun and the Bidassoa valley; Morillo's division only remaining with the army. Happily Wellington was able to say—

---

1. Hope, *Military Memoirs.*
2. Wellington to Bathurst, 21st November, 1813. "The Spaniards began to plunder and did a lot of mischief within the first few days. I sent the Spaniards back into Spain, which has convinced the French of our desire not to injure individuals."

The conduct of the Portuguese and British has been so exactly what I wished, that the natives of this part are not only reconciled to the invasion, but wish us success and afford us all the supplies in their power.[1]

The bridge over the Nive at Cambo, the principal crossing of that river above Bayonne, was some 8 miles up stream from the right of the line held by the allied army in front of Bayonne. The defences of the bridge-head and village were held by Foy's division. On the 14th November Wellington, writing to Hope, said—

The enemy has a bridge at Cambo of which we must deprive him or we shall have no peace during the winter, but we must wait for a fair day or two, and I am desirous of keeping the troops together a little longer in order to hear from England how the Allies in Germany propose to spend the winter.

However, as events turned out no attack was necessary and Wellington got the security he wanted by the action of the French themselves.

As was stated, when dealing with the retreat of the French after the battle on the 10th, Soult on the 12th had placed three divisions under D'Erlon along the right bank of the Nive; but later, in his desire to concentrate his army in the immediate vicinity of Bayonne, he ordered D'Erlon to assemble his troops behind the river about half-way between the city and Cambo, so as to be able to retire rapidly in case of an attack on the fortress, and to watch the river with small parties only.

On the 15th November Soult reconnoitred the right bank of the Nive as far as Cambo. Being, as it appears, impressed by the difficulty of preventing a crossing of the river by the enemy owing to the numerous fords still practicable, notwithstanding the height of the river, and by

---

1. Wellington to Bathurst, 21st November, 1813.

the fact that at many places the left bank had considerable command over the right, he ordered Foy in the presence of D'Erlon to make preparations to destroy the bridge, and to retain on the left bank only from 700 to 800 men who were to retire to the right bank on any attack being made by Hill's troops. Some of the arches of the bridge were of wood, some of stonework.

Foy immediately proceeded to carry out the Marshal's order. At 10 p.m. on the 15th the removal of the guns in the bridge-head works commenced, and by 2 a.m. on the 16th the main body of Foy's division had crossed the river. The sappers then began to mine one of the stone arches and to prepare for burning one of the wooden. But, owing to the firing of a loaded gun in the works by being carelessly spiked, the alarm was given, and Hill's troops got under arms. At daybreak on the 16th, in a fog, the French garrison in the works found the allied outposts within pistol range of the bridge-head. Foy, believing an attack was imminent, sent the garrison across the river, and as soon as they were over, ordered the mine to be fired and the wooden arch set alight. The two arches of the bridge were destroyed, and the allied troops immediately took possession of Cambo.

The Spanish troops having left the army, and Wellington having obtained the security he required, he determined to place the British and Portuguese troops in cantonments, and the necessary order was issued on the 16th November.

The following was the distribution of the army—

Hill's corps to Canton in Itxassou, Cambo, Larressore, Espelette, Ainhoa and Souraide.

The 3rd and 6th Divisions in Ustaritz, Arraunts and adjacents.

The Light Division in rear of Arcangues; the 7th Division in St. Pée.

The 4th Division in Ascain and Serres.

Hope's corps in Bidart, Ahetz, Guethary, and the two brigades of Guards in St. Jean de Luz and Ciboure.

Cavalry, one regiment of Vandeleur's brigade in front of St. Jean de Luz, the rest of the brigade in Urrugne, Hendaye and Biriatou.

Victor Alten's brigade, one regiment in St. Pée, and one in Sare.

Bock's brigade to canton beyond Ernani.

The moves to be made on the 17th November.

General Headquarters at St. Jean de Luz on the 17th.

CHAPTER 21

The Army and the Man

To make one more reference to Sir Henry Bunbury's *Memoirs,* it may be well to state what Wellington's opinion of his army was about this time.

> The Duke said to me, I have the finest army here that man ever commanded. I believe there never was such an army. Not a man or officer ever behaves ill, except—and here he mentioned two unfortunately conspicuous examples—and, he added, the Portuguese troops are nearly as good as the British.[1]

And this army was made by him. From the commencement of his command he had been forming and training it for what he hoped would be its final use, battles on French soil. It was not only its fighting capacity he had raised, but also its moral and spirit, its discipline and its conduct, which was to be such an asset now he had reached France.

This is what an officer, who had served with him in India and the Peninsula, says of the state of the army at this time.

> Latterly nothing could surpass the system of the army. From General to the sentinel everyone seemed to understand his duty perfectly and to practise it without noise or fuss. The Commissariat, certainly not the least important branch of the army, owed its formation and efficiency

1. *Life of Sir H. Bunbury,* by his son.

entirely to his Lordship, and, I believe, it cost him more trouble and annoyance before he could establish it on a good footing than can well be conceived, for, when he first took command of the army in Spain there was not a soul who knew anything about the matter.[1]

Napoleon said that in war "The Man is everything, men are nothing," in other words, however good the troops may be, victory cannot be assured unless a real leader is there to command them. In Wellington the allied army had the Man. On the other hand, however able the Commander, success will not be his unless the troops are brave, staunch and skilful. So what of the men of "that army which recovered the character of the nations of Europe, broke the spell, and induced others to believe they could be successful establishing an imperishable reputation?"[2]

For the most part good honest country men, English, Scots, and Irish, strong and of great endurance—for the weakly soon fell by the way—they were fashioned by regimental discipline and much experience of war into soldiers very formidable, staunch and of great spirit. Their previous successes had given them perfect confidence in themselves, their officers and especially in their great Leader. They knew that in anything like equal numbers they could beat the French whether on the hillside or elsewhere. Not all saints or heroes by any means, but men, no doubt, with many failings, who fought for their country with all their might, and whose courage, constancy and spirit, no one, least of all their foes in the field, have ever questioned. With them must be remembered those Portuguese, brave companions in arms who fought shoulder to shoulder with them in all their fights, and, be it remembered, Wellington throughout was working with an instrument which it behoved him to take the greatest care of, because what he lost of it would

1. Major J. Blakiston, *Twelve Years' Military Adventures*.
2. Sir H. Leith Hay, *A Narrative of the Peninsular War*.

not be replaced for some time, if at all. "We have," he said, "but one army, and if I am to preserve that army I must proceed with caution."

Now of the Man. When he took over the command of the army in Portugal on 27th April, 1809, Wellington was forty years of age. On the 7th July he was appointed Marshal General of the Portuguese Army.

Sir John Moore having been killed in action before Coruna on the 16th January, 1809, there was no general officer in the British Army more fit to take the command in Portugal than Sir Arthur Wellesley, owing to his experience in war and his knowledge of war administration. Detractors might call him the Sepoy General, but it cannot be denied that his service in India had much to do with making him the man he was.

From the various positions he had held in that country he had gained great experience in all matters of civil and military administration, for he was always a thinker and a learner, experience which was to be an asset to him in dealing with not only the problems of his army, but also his dealings with the Portuguese and Spanish governments.

As a Commander in the field he had shown himself to be very bold, very active, though methodical. "Never before in India had armies been so well supplied, so orderly, so strictly disciplined and so rapid in their movements."[1]

For his position as a strategist and tactician we may put the Vitoria campaign and the battle of Salamanca, and to the latter join that piece of beautiful work the crossing of the Bidassoa and capture of the Rhune mountain. Surprise is a deadly foe, it has been said to be the secret of success in war. "No General, not even Napoleon, brought about so many startling surprises as Wellington."[2] It was a favourite weapon of his, and we have seen its success.

Wellington is said to have been a hard man. His watch-

1. Fortescue, *Wellington*.
2. Henderson, *Stonewall Jackson,* Vol. II.

words were Truth and Duty. Now duty is not always easy to carry out or to enforce; from this point of view it may be said that if he had not been hard he could never have made the army what it was. On two points at least he was adamant; he who molested the inhabitants of the country must pay the penalty; and the officer who in action sacrificed the lives of his men whether by carelessness or incompetence must bear his wrath. Himself such a superb handler of troops he could not bear to see or hear of their being mishandled. It was due to his example that throughout the Peninsular Army the highest place in the scale of credit went to him "who did a brilliant deed with little loss."[1]

He was a very sane, very honest, and very well-balanced man, and a tireless worker. Victory did not spoil him, or failure dishearten him. Of wonderful patience, as shown by the constant difficulties he had to meet, he went along steadily towards the goal he had set out for himself. He was blessed with a wonderful eye for ground, and an almost uncanny faculty for judging the characters of the Generals opposed to him and what their actions would be; the moral of troops in action; and the decisive moment in any engagement. When, during the last phase of the battle of Waterloo, even that good soldier Colonel Colborne, with the 52nd, hesitated for a moment in front of the column of the Imperial Guard, he heard the Duke's voice behind him saying quietly, "Go on, Colborne, they won't stand," and the Imperial did not stand. Again, at the battle of Orthez, directly he saw the gap between Taupin's division and that of Rouget he pushed the 52nd into it and gained the day.

We have said that the troops he commanded had perfect confidence in their leader, yet it has been alleged that Wellington cannot be placed in the first line of generals, because he did not secure, or even try to secure, the affection of his soldiers. That was never the motive of his conduct, for he had

1. Kincaid, *Random Shots of a Rifleman.*

quite a different idea of what his duty was, namely not to make himself popular, but to do his duty faithfully and, what was not easy, to make others perform theirs.

No troops ever followed any General with more alacrity, stood fast with more unconquerable determination, or, at his word, started joyously forward into deadly perils, than the British and even the Portuguese soldiers of his army.[1]

On his part Wellington had equal confidence in his men. He knew what they could and could not do, and made his plans accordingly; and he was not ashamed to confess that when he got into a scrape "he trusted to the bravery of his troops to get him out of it."[2]

When the Peninsular War was over there fell to Wellington other scenes of work both military and political. He conquered Napoleon, and by his character, common sense and the power of seeing facts as they were and not as others fancied they were, did more than anyone else to restore order in Europe upset by Napoleon and years of war.

To conclude, we quote Greville's character sketch of him:

In spite of some foibles and faults, he was, beyond all doubt, a very great man—the only great man of the present time—and comparable to the most eminent of those who have lived before him. His greatness was the result of a few striking qualities—a perfect simplicity of character without a particle of vanity or conceit, but with a thorough and strenuous self-reliance, a severe truthfulness, never misled by fancy or exaggeration and an abiding sense of duty and obligation which made him the humblest of citizens and most obedient of subjects. The Crown never had a more faithful, devoted and disinterested subject.[3]

---

1. Hooper, *Wellington*.
2. *Larpent's Journal*.
3. *The Greville Diary*, Vol. I.

Appendices

APPENDIX A

ORDER OF BATTLE OF THE ANGLO-PORTUGUESE ARMY AND OF THE SPANISH TROOPS

UNDER THE COMMAND OF

FIELD-MARSHAL THE MARQUIS OF WELLINGTON

IN OCTOBER, 1813

ANGLO-PORTUGUESE ARMY

STAFF

Commanding the Forces . .	Field-Marshal the Marquis of Wellington, K.G., K.B.
Quartermaster-General . .	Major-General Sir George Murray, K.B.
Adjutant-General . . .	Major-General Hon. E. Pakenham.
Military-Secretary . . .	Lieutenant-Colonel Lord Fitzroy Somerset.
Commanding Royal Artillery .	Lieutenant-Colonel A. Dickson, R.A.
Chief Engineer	Lieutenant-Colonel Elphinstone, R.E.

CIVIL STAFF

Commissary-General . . .	Sir R. Kennedy.
Principal Medical Officer .	Inspector-General J. McGrigor, M.D.
Purveyor-General	Mr. James.
Judge-Advocate	Mr. F. Larpent, Barrister-at-Law.

Lieutenant-General Sir Stapleton Cotton, K.B., Commanding the Cavalry.

CAVALRY BRIGADES

Major-General O'Loghlin (Household Brigade)	1st and 2nd Life Guards. Royal Horse Guards (2 squadrons of each).
Major-General Ponsonby .	5th Dragoon Guards. 3rd Dragoons. 4th Dragoons.
Colonel Grant	13th Light Dragoons. 14th Light Dragoons.
Major-General Vandeleur .	12th Light Dragoons. 16th Light Dragoons.
Major-General Baron Victor Alten	18th Hussars. 1st Hussars, K.G.Legion.
Major-General Bock . . .	1st and 2nd Dragoons, K.G.L.
Major-General Fane . . .	3rd Dragoon Guards. 1st (Royal) Dragoons.
Major-General Lord Edward Somerset (Hussar Brigade)	7th, 10th and 15th Hussars.

PORTUGUESE CAVALRY

Brigadier-General D'Urban .	1st, 6th, 11th and 12th Portuguese Cavalry.
Colonel Campbell	4th Portuguese Cavalry (not brigaded).

The Cavalry brigades were not numbered; in orders they were always designated by the names of their permanent commanders.

All the heavy cavalry and the Portuguese cavalry were in Spain.

ROYAL ARTILLERY

Lieutenant-Colonel A. Dickson commanding.

ROYAL HORSE ARTILLERY

Lieutenant-Colonel A. Frazer commanding.

A (the Chestnut Troop) .	Lieutenant-Colonel H. D. Ross.
D Troop	Captain G. Bean.

E Troop	. . . . .	Major R. W. Gardiner.
F Troop	. . . . .	Lieutenant-Colonel J. Webber Smith.
I Troop	. . . . .	Captain W. Norman Ramsay——Major Bull on sick leave.

FIELD ARTILLERY

Captain L. Carmichael's Battery.
      ,,   W. Greene's   ,,
      ,,   R. Douglas's   ,,
      ,,   C. Mosse's   ,,
      ,,   J. Michell's   ,,
      ,,   T. Brandreth's   ,,
      ,,   R. M. Cairnes'   ,,
Major Sympher's   ,,   K. German Legion.

PORTUGUESE ARTILLERY.——LIEUTENANT-COLONEL TULLOH

Major Cunha's Battery.
Major Arriaga's Battery.
Captain C. Michell's Battery.

HEAVY ARTILLERY

2-gun battery of 18-pounders. Manned by Captains Morrison's and Glubb's Companies.

MOUNTAIN ARTILLERY

A battery of eight 3-pounder guns carried on mules.

Three R.A. Companies and one K.G. Legion Company formed four divisions for gun ammunition supply, and two Companies two divisions for small arm ammunition.

Each Troop and Battery had five guns, 9- or 6-pounders, and one $5\frac{1}{2}$-inch howitzer. The horse artillery troops had generally two 9-pounders and three 6-pounders. The British and German Legion batteries had 9-pounder guns, the Portuguese 6-pounders.

ENGINEERS

5th, 6th, 7th and 8th Companies, Royal Sappers and Miners.

1st Division

Lieutenant-General Hon. Sir John Hope, K.B., commanding a corps.

Major-General Howard, commanding.

Brigades.

1st.—Colonel Maitland. 1/1st and 3/1st Guards and 1 company 5/60th Rifles.

2nd.—Major-General Stopford. 1st Coldstream Guards, 1/3rd Guards, 1 company 5/60th Rifles.

Major-General Hinuber. 1st, 2nd and 5th Line battalions, K.G.L.

Colonel Halket. 1st and 2nd Light battalions, K.G.L.

Aylmer's Brigade.

Major-General Lord Aylmer. 2/62nd, 76th, 77th, 85th.

2nd Division

Lieutenant-General Sir Rowland Hill, K.B., commanding a corps.

Lieutenant-General Hon. Sir W. Stewart, K.B., commanding.

Brigades.

Major-General Walker. 1/50th Foot, 1/71st Highland Light Infantry, 1/92nd Highlanders, 1 company 5/60th Rifles.

Major-General Byng. 1/3rd Foot (the Buffs), 1/57th Foot, 1st Provisional battalion (2/31st and 2/66th), 1 company 5/60th Rifles.

Major-General Pringle. 1/28th, 2/34th, 1/39th regiments, 1 company 5/60th.

Colonel Ashworth. 6th and 18th Portuguese and 6th Caçadores.

3rd Division

Major-General Hon. C. Colville. Lieutenant-General Sir T. Picton being absent on sick leave, but General Brisbane was in command on 7th October, owing to General Colville being in temporary command of the 6th Division.

Brigades.

Major-General Brisbane. 1/45th, 74th Highlanders, 1/88th (Connaught Rangers), Headquarters and 3 companies 5/60th Rifles.

Colonel Keane. 1/5th Fusiliers, 2/83rd, 2/87th, 94th regiments.

Major-General Power. 9th and 21st Portuguese, 11th Caçadores.

4th Division

Lieutenant-General Hon. Sir G. Lowry Cole, K.B., commanding.
Brigades.

Major-General W. Anson. 3/27th, 1/40th, 1/48th regiments, 2nd Provisional battalion (2nd Queen's and 2/53rd).

Major-General Ross. 1/7th Fusiliers, 20th, 1/23rd R. Welsh Fusiliers, 1 company Brunswick Oels.

Colonel Miller, then Colonel Vasconcellos, 11th, 23rd Portuguese, 7th Caçadores.

5th Division

Major-General Hay, commanding during absence of Major-General Oswald, on sick leave.
Brigades.

Colonel Hon. C. Greville. 3/1st Royals, 1/9th, 1/38th, 2/47th, 1 company Brunswick Oels.

Major-General Robinson. 1/4th, 2/59th, 2/84th, 1 company Brunswick Oels.

Colonel de Regoa. 3rd and 5th Portuguese, 8th Caçadores.

6th Division

Major-General Hon. C. Colville in temporary command until the return from sick leave of Lieutenant-General Sir H. Clinton, who commanded on 10th November.
Brigades.

Major-General Pack. 1/42nd Black Watch, 1/79th Highlanders, 1/91st Highlanders, 1 company 5/60th Rifles.

Major-General Lambert. 1/11th, 1/32nd, 1/61st.

Colonel Douglas. 8th and 12th Portuguese, 9th Caçadores.

7th Division

Lieutenant-General the Earl of Dalhousie, K.B. Lord Dalhousie went to England after the crossing of the Bidassoa, when Major-General Le Cor, from the Portuguese brigade, assumed command.
Brigades.

Major-General Barnes. 1/6th, 3rd Provisional battalion (2/24th and 2/58th), 9 companies Brunswick Oels.

Major-General Inglis. 51st, 68th, 1/82nd, Chasseurs Britanniques.

Major-General Le Cor, then Colonel Doyle. 17th and 19th Portuguese.

Light Division

Major-General Baron Charles Alten.

Brigades.

Major-General Kempt. 1/43rd Light Infantry, 1/95th Rifles, 3/95th, 1st Caçadores.

Lieutenant-Colonel Colborne. 1/52nd, 2/95th, 17th Portuguese, 3rd Caçadores.

Portuguese Division

Lieutenant-General Sir J. Hamilton, K.B., commanding.

Brigades.

Brigadier-General Da Costa. 2nd and 14th Portuguese.

Brigadier-General Buchan. 4th and 10th Portuguese, 10th Caçadores.

Independent Portuguese Brigades.

Major-General Bradford. 13th and 24th Portuguese, 5th Caçadores.

Brigadier-General Wilson. 1st and 16th Portuguese, 4th Caçadores.

SPANISH TROOPS

In January, 1813, Wellington had been appointed Generalissimo of the Spanish Armies. Owing, however, to the repeated instances in which the Spanish Government had broken the conditions under which he had accepted the command, Wellington had felt obliged to formally resign it on 30th August, 1813. He received no answer to this until the end of September, when the Spanish War Minister informed him that the Regency accepted his resignation, but desired that he should continue to exercise the command until the question of his resignation was considered by the New Cortes which was about to assemble. This Wellington agreed to do.

In October, 1813, the Spanish troops serving directly under Wellington were:—

The 4th Spanish Army, commanded by Lieutenant-General Don M. Freyre.

Seven regular divisions and the *Guerrilleros* of Navarre, commanded by General Don Espoz y Mina, the Captain-General of that Province.

1st Division, General Don P. Morillo.[1]
2nd   „   General Don Carlos de España.
3rd   „   General Don D. del Barco.
4th   „   General Don P. de Barcena.
5th   „   General Don J. Porlier.
6th   „   General Don F. Longa.
7th   „   General Don G. Mendizabel.

Part of the 7th Division was blockading Santona and Don Carlos's division was besieging Pamplona.

Reserve Army of Andalusia, under General Don P. Giron, two divisions.

3rd Spanish Army, commanded by the Dugue del Parque (succeeded later by the Prince of Angola), which had been moving up from Aragon, arrived at Tudela on 22nd September, and reinforced Don Carlos at Pamplona with one division.

It is difficult to give even approximately what the fighting strength of these troops was. Wellington, in a letter to Sir J. Hope, estimated the strength of a division brought up to St. Jean de Luz as about 4,000. If this figure is taken as a basis, the strengths may be put approximately as follows: —

4th Army, 5 divisions	20,000
Mina's partisans	7,000
Reserve of Andalusia	8,000
3rd Army	12,000
	47,000

[1] Morillo's division was attached to Sir Rowland Hill's corps.

APPENDIX B

2nd November, 1813.

Adjutant-General to General Officers commanding Corps and Divisions.

I have it in command to recall to your attention the expediency of your taking every possible step to impress on all ranks the necessity, as well as the policy, of preserving good order and discipline on the army entering France. General order of the 9th July is to be read on the first three parades after the advance.

It is His Excellency's wish that you should take a favourable opportunity of assembling officers commanding brigades and regiments, and expressing to them His Lordship's peculiar anxiety on the subject, and it is expected you should explain that measures of precaution are to be preferred to those of remedy, as there is hardly a possibility of redressing injuries committed by an uncontrolled soldiery, who, once let out of control, cannot easily be brought under subordination.

H. Pakenham,
Adjutant-General.

To the French. (In French and Basque.)

By Field-Marshal the Marquis of Wellington, General-in-Chief of Allied Armies.

Headquarters.

1st November, 1813.

On entering your country, I announce to you that I have given the most positive orders, a translation of which is given below, to prevent the evils which generally follow invasion by an enemy's army, an invasion which you know was the consequence of that which your government made into Spain, and the successes of the army under my command.

You may rest assured that I will carry out the orders I have given, and I request you to arrest and bring to my headquarters those who, in spite of my orders, do you any injury. But it is necessary on your part that you remain at your houses, and take no part in the war in which your country is about to be the theatre.

APPENDIX C

Fighting strength of the Anglo-Portuguese Army
on 7th October, 1813

State of 7th October, 1813.	Combatant Officers.	Sergeants.	Trumpeters, Buglers and Drummers.	Rank and File.	Total, Exclusive of Officers.	Composition.
Cavalry Division	425	492	133	7,387	8,082	British, German Legion and Portuguese.
1st Infantry Division	236	399	129	6,300	6,828	British and German Legion.
2nd　″　　″	350	479	192	7,271	7,942	British and Portuguese
3rd　″　　″	295	384	193	5,304	5,881	″　　″　　″
4th　″　　″	261	358	143	5,164	5,665	″　　″　　″
5th　″　　″	178	293	119	3,753	4,165	5th Division had heavy losses at San Sebastian, 987 sick and wounded on 7th October.
6th　″　　″	285	358	148	5,400	5,906	British and Portuguese
7th　″　　″	276	296	123	4,760	5,179	″　　″　　″
Light　″　　″	213	292	124	4,336	4,752	″　　″　　″
Aylmer's Brigade .	100	112	43	1,662	1,817	British.
Portuguese Division	137	222	76	4,194	4,492	Portuguese.
Bradford's Brigade	76	138	64	1,863	2,065	″
Wilson's Brigade .	64	120	29	1,595	1,744	″
Total Infantry	2,471	3,451	1,383	51,602	56,436	
Artillery . . .	153	―	―	―	4,355	State, 25th September
Engineers . . .	40	―	―	―	360	″　　″　　″
Staff Corps . . .	19	―	―	―	328	″　　″　　″
	212	―	―	―	5,043	
Total, all Arms	3,108	―	―	―	69,561	

In addition to the above there were on this date:

Sick and wounded 20,174
On Command 6,710

As the sergeants, drummers and buglers carried no firearms, except in the Rifle battalions, the strength of the rank and file gives practically the number of rifles and muskets which could be brought into action.

APPENDIX D

Strength of the Anglo–Portuguese Army, commanded by Field-Marshal the Marquis of Wellington from June to November, 1813. The 77th Regiment and the Royal Veteran battalion, both at Lisbon, the 1st Guards brigade at Oporto owing to sickness until 18th August, and all men missing and prisoners of war still on the strength of their units, are omitted.

	Fighting Strength present with Units and fit for Duty.		Sick and Wound-ed.	On Com-mand.	
	Com-batant Offi-cers.	Other Ranks.			
State of 17th June before Battle of Vitoria.					The figures under the heading "On Command" denote the numbers of N.C. Officers and Men detached from their units on special employment, such as serving in the Staff Corps, as assistants to the Provost Marshal, as Orderlies and batmen to General and Staff Officers. But the larger parts of the figures consist of men employed in the general hospitals and convalescent depots behind the Army, as wardmasters, storekeepers and attendants, because there was then no Medical Corps for such duties.
British Cavalry .	327	6,821	495	826	
Portuguese ,, .	111	1,552	280	248	
Total ,, .	438	8,373	775	1,074	
British Infantry .	1,681	38,564	8,725	2,165	
Portuguese ,, .	983	25,904	4,969	1,679	
Total ,, .	2,664	64,468	13,694	3,844	
Royal Horse Artillery . . .	23	780	75	51	From state of 25th May, 1813.
Field Artillery: British, German Legion and Portuguese	132	3,395	495	879	,,　　,,　　,,　　,,
Royal Engineers .	41	304	35	74	,,　　,,　　,,　　,,
Staff Corps of Cavalry, The Military Police of the Army . . .	20	213	56	—	,,　　,,　　,,　　,,
Total . .	216	4,692	661	1,004	
Total, all Arms .	3,318	77,533	15,130	5,922	

Fighting Strength Anglo-Portuguese Army. Present and fit for Duty.	Combatant Officers.	Other Ranks.	Sick and Wounded.	On Command.	
Morning State, 16th July, 1813					
British Cavalry .	308	6,335	764	954	The British and Portuguese casualties in action from 21st June to 8th July were 297 Officers and 4,178 other ranks, of whom 33 Officers and 688 other ranks were killed. On 16th July the decrease in the fighting strength was 1,044 other ranks. Increase in sick and wounded, 6,254.
Portuguese ,, .	98	1,408	165	469	
Total ,, .	406	7,743	929	1,423	
British Infantry .	1,691	32,152	12,381	2,664	
Portuguese ,, .	848	23,243	7,377	2,241	
Total ,, .	2,529	55,395	19,758	4,905	
Horse and Field Artillery . .	158	3,949	632	1,118	State of 25th July.
Royal Engineers and Staff Corps	43	506	68	74	,, ,, ,,
Total, all Arms	3,136	67,087	21,387	7,520	
Morning State, 8th August, 1813					
British Cavalry .	304	6,482	682	804	The British and Portuguese casualties in action from 9th July to 2nd August inclusive were 365 Officers and 7,889 other ranks, of whom 72 Officers and 2,009 others were killed or missing. Practically all these losses were in the infantry, as out of the 7,050 casualties during the fighting in the Pyrenees, the only other casualties were 2 General Staff Officers killed and 7 wounded, 6 artillery men wounded and 1 cavalryman missing. Further decrease in fighting strength, 8,140. State of 25th August.
Portuguese ,, .	89	1,349	155	487	
Total ,, .	393	7,831	837	1,291	
British Infantry .	1,386	26,570	14,558	3,112	
Portuguese ,, .	842	20,402	8,103	2,235	
Total ,, .	2,228	46,972	22,661	5,347	
Artillery, Engineers and Staff Corps . . .	209	4,144	691	1,145	
Total, all Arms	2,830	58,947	24,189	7,783	
Morning State, 8th September, 1813					
British Cavalry .	320	6,264	647	1,123	The casualties in action from 3rd to 31st August were 195 Officers and 3,139 others, of whom 45 Officers and 724 others were killed. But the 1st Guards Brigade (58 Officers and 1,688 other ranks) rejoined the 1st Infantry Division on 18th August, Aylmer's brigade (120 officers, 1,949 other ranks) was taken on the strength on 22nd August, and about 800 men in drafts arrived from England. The wounded at Vitoria were now beginning to rejoin their units, and the infantry fighting strength was increased by 7,082. Writing to the Secretary of State on 25th August Wellington said : " We are getting some men from the hospitals every day, and I do not doubt we are now as strong as we were on 25th July."
Portuguese ,, .	93	1,360	161	394	
Total ,, .	413	7,624	808	1,517	
British Infantry .	1,649	32,645	14,207	2,548	
Portuguese ,, .	861	21,409	7,526	1,707	
Total ,, .	2,510	54,054	21,733	4,255	
Artillery, Engineers and Staff Corps . . .	213	4,712	842	1,049	
Total, all Arms	3,136	66,390	23,583	6,828	

Fighting Strength, Anglo-Portuguese Army. Present and fit for Duty.	Combatant Officers.	Other Ranks.	Sick and Wounded.	On Command.	
Morning State, 7th October, 1813					
British Cavalry .	332	6,772	611	723	Increase in infantry strength, 2,382.
Portuguese ,, .	93	1,310	106	415	
Total ,, .	425	8,082	717	1,138	Decrease in sick and wounded, 3,409.
British Infantry .	1,699	34,188	13,323	2,714	
Portuguese ,, .	772	22,248	5,443	1,802	
Total ,, .	2,471	56,436	18,766	4,516	
Artillery, Engineers and Staff Corps . . .	212	5,043	691	1,056	State, 25th September.
Total, all Arms	3,108	69,561	20,174	6,710	
Morning State, 5th November, 1813					The casualties in action on 7th and 8th October were 44 Officers and 774 other ranks, killed, wounded and missing.
British Cavalry .	392	8,004	527	595	
Portuguese ,, .	107	1,316	103	443	
Total ,, .	499	9,320	630	1,038	Increase in infantry strength, 1,092; in sick and wounded, 87; decrease in " On Command," 383.
British Infantry .	1,743	34,764	12,989	2,614	
Portuguese ,, .	806	22,764	5,875	1,635	
Total ,, .	2,549	57,528	18,864	4,247	
Artillery, Engineers and Staff Corps . . .	210	4,084	767	1,042	State, 25th October.
Total, all Arms	3,258	70,932	20,261	6,327	

APPENDIX E

ORDER OF BATTLE OF THE ARMY OF SPAIN

IST OCTOBER, 1813

Commanding-in-Chief . .	Maréchal Soult, Duc de Dalmatie.
Chief of the Staff	Lieutenant-Général Count Gazan.
Commanding the Artillery .	Général de division Tirlet.
Chief Engineer	Général de division Levy.
Commissary Général . . .	M. Favier.
Surgeon-in-Chief	Rapatal.

CAVALRY

1st Division

Général de division, Baron P. Soult.

Brigades.
Générals de brigade, Berton, Vinot, and Sparre.   Strength, present and fit for duty, 3,901.[1]

2nd Division (Heavy Cavalry)

Général de division, Treilhard.

Brigades.
Générals Ismert and Ormancey.   Strength, 2,312.

Total Cavalry—6,213.

INFANTRY

Right Wing of Army.   Lieutenant-Général Count Reille.

1st Division

Général de division, Foy.
This division was detached to the extreme left of the army.
Brigades.
Fririon and Berlier.   Fighting strength, 4,654.

[1] In the French states officers are included in the totals.

219

7th Division

Général de division, Maucune, replaced later by Général Leval.
Brigades.
Pinoteau and Montfort.   Strength, 3,996.

9th Division

Général de brigade, Boyer.   He had succeeded to the command
of the division *vice* Lamartinière, killed in action on 1st September.
His brigade was commanded by the Senior Colonel.
Brigades.
Gauthier and ———.   Strength, 6,515.
Total strength of Right Wing without Foy's division, 10,551.
Centre of the Army.   Lieutenant-Général Baron Clausel.

4th Division

Général de division, Baron Conroux.

Brigades.
Rey and Baurot.   Strength, 4,962.

5th Division

Général de division, Maransin.

Brigades.
Barbot and Rouget.   Strength, 5,575.

8th Division

Général de division, Taupin.

Brigades.
Bechaud and Dein.   Bechaud wounded on 7th October, replaced
by Colonel Dauture.   Strength, 4,778.
Total strength Centre of Army, 15,315.
Artillery, 18 guns.
Left Wing of Army.   Lieutenant-Général Count D'Erlon.

2nd Division

Général de division, Darmagnac.

Brigades.
Chassé and Gruardet.   Strength, 4,447.

3rd Division

Général de division, Abbé.

Brigades.
Boivin and Maucomble.   Strength, 6,051.

6th Division

Général de division, Darricau.

Brigades.
Saint Pol and Mocquery.   Strength, 4,092.
Total strength of Left Wing, 14,590.
Artillery, 20 guns.

Reserve Division

Général de division, Villatte, had four brigades.
French Brigade.   Jamin.
Spanish Brigade.   Casabianca.
Italian Brigade.   Saint Paul.
German Brigade.   Krause.
Strength, 8,018.

Total fighting strength of Army:——
Cavalry.	6,213
Infantry	53,088
Artillery, Engineers, and Gendarmerie, etc. .	8,530

Total   67,831

The garrisons of the fortresses of Bayonne, Navarrenx, St. Jean Pied-de-Port, Pamplona and Santona amounted to 8,711 on 1st October, 1813.

www.ingramcontent.com/pod-product-compliance
Lightning Source LLC
Chambersburg PA
CBHW032053080426
42733CB00006B/261